First World War
and Army of Occupation
War Diary
France, Belgium and Germany

61 DIVISION
Divisional Troops
Royal Army Medical Corps
2/3 South Midland Field Ambulance
1 December 1915 - 28 July 1919

WO95/3051/3

The Naval & Military Press Ltd
www.nmarchive.com
Published in association with The National Archives

Published by

The Naval & Military Press Ltd

Unit 10 Ridgewood Industrial Park,

Uckfield, East Sussex,

TN22 5QE England

Tel: +44 (0) 1825 749494

www.naval-military-press.com

www.nmarchive.com

This diary has been reprinted in facsimile from the original. Any imperfections are inevitably reproduced and the quality may fall short of modern type and cartographic standards.

© **Crown Copyright**
Images reproduced by permission of The National Archives, London, England, 2015.

Contents

Document type	Place/Title	Date From	Date To
Heading	2/3rd South Midland Field Ambulance		
Heading	61st Division 2-3rd Sth Mid. Fld Amb. 1915 Sep-1919 Jly		
War Diary	Chelmsford	00/09/1915	00/10/1915
War Diary	Brentwood	00/11/1915	00/11/1915
Heading	War Diary of 2nd/3rd South Midland Field Ambulance. From 1st December 1915, To 31st December 1915 Volume 2		
War Diary	Brentwood	01/12/1915	31/12/1915
War Diary	War Diary of 2/3rd South Midland Field Amb. From Jan 1916 To Jan 31 1916		
War Diary	Brentwood	01/01/1916	31/01/1916
War Diary	Ref May.108.05		
War Diary	Upminster Common		
War Diary	Billericay		
War Diary	Upminster Common		
War Diary	Ingrave		
Heading	61st Division 2/3rd S.M. Field Ambulance May 1916		
War Diary	Perham Down Salisbury Plain	01/05/1916	31/05/1916
Heading	61st Division 2/3 S.M. Field Ambulance June 1916		
War Diary	Robecq	01/06/1916	11/06/1916
War Diary	La. Gorgue	12/06/1916	30/06/1916
Heading	War Diary Of 2/3rd S.M. Field Ambulance 61st Division July 1916 Volume.3		
War Diary	La Gorgue	01/07/1916	07/07/1916
War Diary	Vielle Chapelle	07/07/1916	15/07/1916
War Diary	La Gorque	16/07/1916	31/07/1916
Heading	War Diary 2/3 S.M. Field Ambulance Volume 4		
War Diary	La Gorgue	01/08/1916	31/08/1916
Heading	War Diary 2/3rd (S.M) Field Ambulance 61st Div September 1916 Volume 5.		
War Diary	La Gorgue 36 A. L.35b.9.9.	01/09/1916	30/09/1916
Heading	61st Division 2/3 S.M Field Ambulance Oct 1916		
War Diary	La Gorgue	02/10/1916	28/10/1916
War Diary	Le Cornet	29/10/1916	31/10/1916
Heading	War Diary 2/3rd S.M. Field Ambulance 61st Division Period 1. 30. November 1916 Volume 7		
War Diary	Raimbert	01/11/1916	01/11/1916
War Diary	Rocourt	02/11/1916	02/11/1916
War Diary	Guestreville	03/11/1916	04/11/1916
War Diary	Maisnil St Pol	05/11/1916	05/11/1916
War Diary	Boffles	06/11/1916	14/11/1916
War Diary	Le Meillard	15/11/1916	15/11/1916
War Diary	La Haie Farm	16/11/1916	16/11/1916
War Diary	La Vlcoqyne	17/11/1916	17/11/1916
War Diary	Warloy	18/11/1916	18/11/1916
War Diary	Martinsart	19/11/1916	22/11/1916
War Diary	Cabstand	23/11/1916	27/11/1916
War Diary	Varennes	28/11/1916	30/11/1916

Heading	War Diary 2/3 S.M Field Ambulance December 1916 Volume 8		
War Diary	Varennes	01/12/1916	31/12/1916
Heading	War Diary 2/3 S.M. Field Ambulance 61st Division January 1917 Volume 9		
War Diary	Varennes	01/01/1917	15/01/1917
War Diary	Beauquesnes	16/01/1917	16/01/1917
War Diary	Le Meillard	17/01/1917	17/01/1917
War Diary	Conteville	18/01/1917	18/01/1917
War Diary	L'abbaye D'aimont Farm	19/01/1917	31/01/1917
Heading	War Diary of 2/3 Field Ambulance 61st Divn. From February 1st 1917 To February 28th 1917 (Volume 10)		
War Diary	L'abbaye D'aimont Farm	01/02/1917	03/02/1917
War Diary	L'Etoile	04/02/1917	13/02/1917
War Diary	Marcelcave	13/02/1917	16/02/1917
War Diary	Harbonnieres	16/02/1917	28/02/1917
Heading	War Diary Of The 2/3rd Field Ambulance March 1 To 31 1917		
War Diary	Harbonnieres	01/03/1917	29/03/1917
War Diary	Falvy	30/03/1917	31/03/1917
Heading	War Diary of 2/3rd South Midland Field Ambulance From April 1st 1917 To April 30th 1917		
War Diary	Falvy	01/04/1917	02/04/1917
War Diary	Trefcon	03/04/1917	10/04/1917
War Diary	Douilly	11/04/1917	20/04/1917
War Diary	Foreste	21/04/1917	30/04/1917
Heading	War Diary of 2/3 S.M. Field Ambulance From 1/5/17 To 31/5/17		
War Diary	Foreste	01/05/1917	31/05/1917
Miscellaneous	Appendix I 3rd Field Ambulance.		
Miscellaneous	Appendix II Specification to R.E. for Dug-out Dressing Stations at Posts:-		
Miscellaneous	Appendix III "A" Section. 3rd Field Ambulance. "A" pannier.		
War Diary	Arras	01/06/1917	09/06/1917
War Diary	Simencourt	10/06/1917	20/06/1917
War Diary	Oeuf	21/06/1917	30/06/1917
Miscellaneous	Appendix 1 Particulars of those carried during the move on June 22nd. 1917.	22/06/1917	22/06/1917
Miscellaneous	Appendix IV A.F.W. 3210, Use of.		
Miscellaneous	Appendix V To. A.D.M.S., 61st. Division.	02/05/1917	02/05/1917
Miscellaneous	Appendix VI 3rd. Field Ambulance.	17/05/1917	17/05/1917
Heading	War Diary of 2/3rd South Midland Field Ambulance From June 1st 1917 To June 30th 1917		
Heading	War Diary of 2/3rd South Midland Field Ambulance From July 1st 1917 To July 31st 1917		
Miscellaneous	Summary Of Medical War Diaries Of 2/3rd S.M.F.A.		
War Diary	Oeuf	01/07/1917	25/07/1917
War Diary	Zeggers Cappel	26/07/1917	31/07/1917
Heading	War Diary of 2/3rd South Midland Field Ambulance From August 1st 1917 To August 31st 1917		
Miscellaneous	Summary Of Medical War Diaries Of 2/3rd S.M.F.A		
War Diary	Peenhoff Farm	01/08/1917	14/08/1917
War Diary	Mill farm L.13.d.32 Map 27	16/08/1917	16/08/1917
War Diary	Goldfish Chateau H. 10. D.28 Map 28.	17/08/1917	17/08/1917
War Diary	Wieltje ADS	17/08/1917	31/08/1917

Heading	War Diary of 2/3rd South Midland Field Ambulance From September 1st 1917 To September 30th 1917 (Volume)		
Miscellaneous	2/3rd (S.M.) F. A. 61st Div. Corps.		
War Diary	Wieltje Mine Shaft ADS	01/09/1917	07/09/1917
War Diary	Wieltje ADS C28a95 Sheet 28	09/09/1917	14/09/1917
War Diary	Watou No 2 Area L19.b.38 Sheet 27	15/09/1917	16/09/1917
War Diary	Le Nouveau Monde I. 11a. Sheet 27	17/09/1917	19/09/1917
War Diary	Simen Court Q10 Sheet 51c	20/09/1917	20/09/1917
War Diary	Arras G22b 0.5 Sheet 51b	21/09/1917	30/09/1917
Heading	War Diary of 2/3rd South Midland Field Ambulance From October 1st 1917 To October 31st. 1917		
War Diary	Arras	01/10/1917	31/10/1917
Heading	War Diary of 2/3rd South Midland Field Ambulance From 1st November 1917 To 30th November 1917		
War Diary	Arras Sheet 51B G22.b.0.3.	01/11/1917	30/11/1917
War Diary	Havrincourt Wood Q15.a.7.5. Sheet 57c	30/11/1917	30/11/1917
Heading	War Diary of 2/3rd South Midland Field Ambulance From December 1st. 1917 To December 31st 1917		
War Diary	Havrincourt Wood Q15.Sheet 57c	01/12/1917	01/12/1917
War Diary	Metz Q20. Sheet 57c	02/12/1917	03/12/1917
War Diary	Fins V12a 91 Sheet 57c	03/12/1917	05/12/1917
War Diary	V11b4.4. Sheet 57c	06/12/1917	24/12/1917
War Diary	Bray	24/12/1917	31/12/1917
War Diary	Marcelcave	31/12/1917	31/12/1917
Heading	War Diary of 2/3rd South Midland Field Ambulance From January 1st 1918 To January 31st 1918		
War Diary	Marcelcave Sheet Amiens G2	01/01/1918	05/01/1918
War Diary	Roye (Sheet. St Amiens J.4)	07/01/1918	07/01/1918
War Diary	Germaine Sheet. St Quentin B.3	09/01/1918	10/01/1918
War Diary	Germaine E17b2.8 Sheet 66d	10/01/1918	31/01/1918
Heading	War Diary of 2/3rd South Midland Field Ambulance From 1st February 1918 To 28th February 1918		
War Diary	Germaine Map Ref E7a2.8 Sheet 66d	01/02/1918	28/02/1918
Heading	War Diary of 2/3rd South Midland Field Ambulance From March 1st 1918 To March 31st 1918		
War Diary	Germaine E17a28 Sheet 66d	01/03/1918	22/03/1918
War Diary	Marche Allouarde Sheet 66d N4c1.1	22/03/1918	24/03/1918
War Diary	Fransart G8d42 Sheet 66d	24/03/1918	25/03/1918
War Diary	Warvillers (Sheet Amiens) I3.24	25/03/1918	26/03/1918
War Diary	Morisel (Sheet Amiens) 3F6.3	26/03/1918	28/03/1918
War Diary	Hailles 3F7.7	27/03/1918	28/03/1918
War Diary	Gentelles (Amiens) 2F5.2	28/03/1918	31/03/1918
War Diary	Boves (Amiens) 2E5.2	31/03/1918	31/03/1918
Heading	War Diary of 2/3rd South Midland Field Ambulance From April 1st 1918 To April 31st 1918		
War Diary	Boves (Amiens 17) 2E5.2	01/04/1918	02/04/1918
War Diary	Picquigny (Amiens.17) 1By.B	03/04/1918	03/04/1918
War Diary	St. Mavlvis (Dieppe 16) Qk 1.8	04/04/1918	11/04/1918
War Diary	St. Venant Sheet 36a P.a.b.	11/04/1918	12/04/1918
War Diary	Guarbecque O11.c.5.8 Sheet 36a	12/04/1918	19/04/1918
War Diary	Lambres N.10.b. Sheet 36a	20/04/1918	30/04/1918
Heading	War Diary of 2/3rd South Midland Field Ambulance From 1st May 1918 To 31st May 1918		
War Diary	Lambres N.10.b.6.1. Sheet 36a	02/05/1918	30/05/1918

Heading	War Diary of 2/3rd South Midland Field Ambulance From 1st June 1918 To 30th June 1918		
War Diary	Lambres N. 10.b.6.0 Sheet 36a	01/06/1918	15/06/1918
War Diary	Berguette O.16.c.6.6.	17/06/1918	20/06/1918
War Diary	Berguette O16c6.6 Sheet 36a	21/06/1918	30/06/1918
Heading	War Diary of 2/3rd South Midland Field Ambulance From 1st July 1918 To 31st July 1918		
War Diary	Berguette O.16.c.6.6. Sheet 36a	01/07/1918	11/07/1918
War Diary	Bourecq U.1c.3.6 Sheet 36a	12/07/1918	18/07/1918
War Diary	Rincq H.19.d.9.9. Sheet 36a	19/07/1918	22/07/1918
War Diary	Quiestede A28.b.1.3	23/07/1918	31/07/1918
Heading	War Diary of 2/3rd South Midland Field Ambulance From 1st August 1918 To 31st August 1918		
War Diary	Fontes N29b 30a Sheet 36c	01/08/1918	05/08/1918
War Diary	Boeseghem I7d 8c Sheet 36a	06/08/1918	24/08/1918
War Diary	Haverskerque J28d 48	25/08/1918	31/08/1918
Heading	War Diary of 2/3rd South Midland Field Ambulance From 1st September 1918 To 30th September 1918		
War Diary	Haverskerque J28d 48 Sheet 36c	01/09/1918	03/09/1918
War Diary	L22c28	04/09/1918	08/09/1918
War Diary	L22c28 Sheet 36a	09/09/1918	30/09/1918
Heading	War Diary of 2/3rd South Midland Field Ambulance From 1st October 1918 To 31st October 1918		
War Diary	L.22.c.2.8.	01/10/1918	03/10/1918
War Diary	Steenbecque	04/10/1918	06/10/1918
War Diary	Beaurepaire	06/10/1918	09/10/1918
War Diary	Doullens	09/10/1918	09/10/1918
War Diary	J.7.c. Cent Map57c	10/10/1918	16/10/1918
War Diary	Cambrai A.16.a.7.2 Sheet57b	17/10/1918	31/10/1918
Heading	War Diary of 2/3rd South Midland Field Ambulance From 1st November 1918 To 30th November 1918		
War Diary	Cambrai College Notre Dame De Grace	01/11/1918	23/11/1918
War Diary	Haplincourt Sheet Lensil. L.5.	24/11/1918	24/11/1918
War Diary	Albert	25/11/1918	30/11/1918
Heading	War Diary of 2/3rd South Midland Field Ambulance From 1st December 1918 To 31st December 1918		
War Diary	Albert (Lens 6H81)	01/12/1918	01/12/1918
War Diary	Puchevillers Lens	03/12/1918	06/12/1918
War Diary	Bernaville 5.B.9.6	07/12/1918	07/12/1918
War Diary	Mesnil Domqueur 5A 9.6	08/12/1918	08/12/1918
War Diary	Domart 6B59	09/12/1918	17/12/1918
War Diary	Domart-En-Ponthieu (Lens 6B59)	19/12/1918	27/12/1918
War Diary	Domart (Lens 6B59)	28/12/1918	31/12/1918
Heading	War Diary of 2/3rd South Midland Field Ambulance From 1st January 1919 To 31st January 1919		
War Diary	Domart En Ponthieu (Lens.6B59)	01/01/1919	30/01/1919
Heading	War Diary of 2/3rd South Midland Field Ambulance From 1st February To 28th February 1919		
War Diary	Domart-En-Ponthieu (Lens 6B59)	01/02/1918	11/02/1918
War Diary	Bussus-Bussuel (Abbeville 5L93)	12/02/1918	28/02/1918
Heading	War Diary of 2/3rd South Midland Field Ambulance From March 1st 1919 To March 31st 1919		
War Diary	Bussus Bussuel Maps Abbeville.14 Lens II.	01/03/1919	26/03/1919
War Diary	Le Treport	27/03/1919	31/03/1919
Heading	War Diary of 2/3rd South Midland Field Ambulance From 1st April 1919 To 30th April 1919		

War Diary	Le Treport	01/04/1919	30/04/1919
Heading	2/3rd S. Mid. Field Amb.		
War Diary	Le Treport	01/05/1919	25/05/1919
Heading	2/3 8th. Mid. 7. 0.		
War Diary	Le Preport	01/06/1919	27/06/1919
Heading	2/3rd Sth. Mid. F.A. July 1919		
War Diary	Le Treport	03/07/1919	28/07/1919

Bri (Brian)
South Midlands
Fizzy Ambulance.

61ST DIVISION

2-3RD STH MID. FLD AMB.

~~IV 1915-DEC 1918~~

1915 SEP — 1919 JLY

Army Form C. 2118.

WAR DIARY
or
INTELLIGENCE SUMMARY.
(Erase heading not required.)

2/3 Field Amb

Hour, Date, Place	Summary of Events and Information	Remarks and references to Appendices
Chelmsford. Sept 1915.	The 3rd Feld Amb continued training in Chelmsford. The main feature in the past month has been the intensive training in Punjab field exercises which have on a rule been held twice a week. Apart from the innovation & particulars, amput, the exercises have also neither valuable & particularly useful. The reason being that owing to the unavoidable long delays in getting between getting the troops into position and the return of information that certain casualties have been made. the jed amb. has little or nothing to do beyond preparing some dressing station. The training of men to find casualties & first aid and carry the wounded back to the wagon and in the preparations of a dressing station can be more htter accomplished when the field amb. works alone. In addition to the field days, this work is generally done twice a week, and the men can get more	

WAR DIARY
or
INTELLIGENCE SUMMARY.
(Erase heading not required.)

Army Form C. 2118.

Hour, Date, Place	Summary of Events and Information	Remarks and references to Appendices

Instruction and supervision there than on a field day.

As a rule field days end where the work of manoeuvre
Corps would be about beginning in real warfare,
and our experience is that no reserve Sec. officers
information to act to the position of troops to send
the known out. When the Staff fat wounds.
Our experience of the officers he made is different.
They are pair experience in map reading. Writing
orders. Selection of suitable places for dressing stations and
the this the work has been valuable.
The transport was inspected during the months and
satisfied the Officer.
Usefull lectures in Hospitals were continues on

Army Form C. 2118.

WAR DIARY
or
INTELLIGENCE SUMMARY.
(Erase heading not required.)

Instructions regarding War Diaries and Intelligence Summaries are contained in F.S. Regs., Part II. and the Staff Manual respectively. Title pages will be prepared in manuscript.

Hour, Date, Place	Summary of Events and Information	Remarks and references to Appendices
	Oatlands, and the men are returning the recruits and compact of cleanliness is visible. One cook has been for a course of training. The general health has been excellent.	

B. Joyce Lt(W)
O.C. 3rd Reserve
G. Div

WAR DIARY
INTELLIGENCE SUMMARY.
(Erase heading not required.)

Army Form C. 2118.

Hour, Date, Place	Summary of Events and Information	Remarks and references to Appendices
October. 1915. Chelmsford.	During the month past, the training has been continued on the same lines as in previous months. Several Divisional and Brigade tactical exercises have been taken then part in, and whole initiative to officers in field work. afford little scope for work further than beyond what ones be done in a day's work by themselves. The marching of the men and the driving has been good - few falls out, and the transport kept their distances with and manage to have men under satisfactorily. Equipment about the same as last month. There have/little news. On Oct 26. 150 limit marched to Brentwood. and	

Took possession of the dinner school near the station. The place was very suitable in many ways but was little prepared for the accommodation of troops. The major portion of the stairs were hardly begun & ffurnitts [?] and iron bound, and sun were unfinished a fortnight after. # Stellenbosch has but poor furniture here. The difficulties seem to be[?] very number of troops in the small town. After only a few days after getting in. a heavy fall of rain strained[?] the basement. and rain came through the roof in many places.
Efficient orderly hours (O.) have been supplied.

B. Rogers Lt.N[?]
OC. 3? December Sm[?]

3rd S.M. Durands
G.S.

Army Form C. 2118.

WAR DIARY
or
INTELLIGENCE SUMMARY.
(Erase heading not required.)

Instructions regarding War Diaries and Intelligence Summaries are contained in F.S. Regs., Part II. and the Staff Manual respectively. Title pages will be prepared in manuscript.

Hour, Date, Place	Summary of Events and Information	Remarks and references to Appendices
November 1915 Fort Road Iron	During the month the Unit has been stationed in Drentwood. Its men being in an empty Industrial School. Left and officers in billets. Horses in billet on S. side of railway in sheds (wooden) and other buildings. German demonstrating. Gunnery has been continued with some time at Lud.Jne. Suggest that use has been made of the hundreds of mountaineering. It has been to practice filling, fuzing, obturating fuses. One of No Coys ... Sgt J Kenyshan benelled at the beginning of the month. Sickness amongst horses present one case. which proved fatal. Great difficulty was experienced in getting Equipment for the Kits. Much did not come till 2 weeks after	

WAR DIARY
INTELLIGENCE SUMMARY
(Erase heading not required.)

Army Form C. 2118.

3 Field Amb'ce Div

Hour, Date, Place	Summary of Events and Information	Remarks and references to Appendices
November 1915 Sevenderood	of sea incidents. He hopes as train on board the same applies to travel equipment, and new uses his intercom (Sec 5.) Had the border been anticipated too and would have pitin Gibeli Austria in one house, which would have saved a great deal of bother and inconvenience. Tonight horses have been over colder to the port — death of men food. Sent ashore to Voorduine one to Cambridge in board on Egra. Anthony Bowley Lt. Col. O/C 3rd Fld. Amb. 61st (8th. Mid.) Division.	

Confidential

War Diary
of
2nd/3rd South Midland Field Ambulance.
from 1st December 1915 to 31st December 1915

Volume 2.

2/3 Sn Hhants.

Army Form C. 2118.

WAR DIARY
or
INTELLIGENCE SUMMARY.
(Erase heading not required.)

Instructions regarding War Diaries and Intelligence Summaries are contained in F. S. Regs., Part II. and the Staff Manual respectively. Title pages will be prepared in manuscript.

1915

Place	Date	Hour	Summary of Events and Information	Remarks and references to Appendices
BRENTWOOD	Dec 1	9-12 / 2-4 pm	Sp they. No. 30 F.S. 2 m to 1 march. Stations moving on site. Communion & Chaplain (Capt BEARD).	
"	" 2	9.3.	Collection of accoutrements route march.	
"	" 3	9-12 / 2-4 pm	Station inspection. Rapid & musical inspection. Pay Parade	
"	" 4			
"	" 5	9. am.	Church Parade from Brentwood Ch. & chapel.	
"	" 6	9-12 / 2-4 pm	Demonstration of Parade. Route march.	
"	" 7	9-12 / 2-4 pm	Spar & Stretcher Ph. #	App I.
"	" 8	9-3	Pay reading lecture. Subject practice.	
"	" 9	9-12	Stretcher Ph. Bandaging, no flesh. Arms Dalgen re accident to M. FOLEY'S CART.	
"	" 10	9-3 / 4pm	Route march. Pay Parade	
"	" 11	9-12	General cleaning of transport material inspection.	
"	" 12	9. am	Church & memorial parade	
"	" 13	9-12	Route march. Bringing Hillier & Brigade.	

2/3 Sn Helmut

Army Form C. 2118.

WAR DIARY
or
INTELLIGENCE SUMMARY.
(Erase heading not required.)

Instructions regarding War Diaries and Intelligence Summaries are contained in F.S. Regs, Part II. and the Staff Manual respectively. Title pages will be prepared in manuscript.

1915 Place	Date	Hour	Summary of Events and Information	Remarks and references to Appendices
PORTSMOUTH	Dec 14	9-3	Gell Iperation. Collection of records.	Ap I
"	" 15	9-12	Sketches & map service	
			Brig A. 773 re leave.	
"	" 16	9-12	Route march.	Ap II
		2-4	Drawing	
			LIEUT F MAYE S. joined unit.	Ap III
"	" 17	9-16	Squad drills	
		10-11	Lecture	
		3	Brig Reynolds. Troop transport men transferred to O.T.C.	
"	" 18	9-10	Medical Inspection.	
		10-12	Route march.	
			Brig. Ad. 756 re Divn.	
			CAPT. J. McCLANNAHAN m Gen. Dec 14. "Services available on mobilization"	
"	" 19	9.	Church & nonconformists Parade.	
"	" 20	9-12	Route march.	
		2.4	Drawing.	
"	" 21	9-12	Reports helps of Probal. Examination of all men & kits.	
			Some British forms in cooler room.	

2/3 Sm Rsah

Army Form C. 2118.

WAR DIARY
or
INTELLIGENCE SUMMARY.
(Erase heading not required.)

Place	1915 Date	Hour	Summary of Events and Information	Remarks and references to Appendices
BRENTWOOD	Sep 22	9-12	Enquiry into kifpn. 5 men instructed ment.	JB
"		9-12	Route march	
"	" 23		Stretcher examination	JB
			G.O.C. Forces to troops in rifle.	
			O.C. v. MAJOR (PRIEL) on leave. CAPT F BOUCHER takes Command.	JB
			LT. F. MAYES' name in Gazette.	
"	" 24	9-12	Brennchamp & medical inspection.	JB
		3 pm	Pay Parade.	JB
"	" 25	9 am	Church & horsemanship parade.	JB
"	" 26	9	Churches assignment parade.	JB
"	" 27	9-12	Route march.	JB
			O.C. return from leave & resumes Command.	
			Courtmartial applied for 5 men charged with theft.	
"	" 28	9-3	Field operations.	JB	Appendix IV.
"	" 29	9-12	Route march. Brennen orders by men.	JB
"	" 30	9-3	During oblision & Collection of wounded.	JB	Appendix V.

2/3 Bn 1st Aunts

Army Form C. 2118.

Instructions regarding War Diaries and Intelligence Summaries are contained in F. S. Regs., Part II. and the Staff Manual respectively. Title pages will be prepared in manuscript.

WAR DIARY
or
INTELLIGENCE SUMMARY.
(Erase heading not required.)

Place	Date	Hour	Summary of Events and Information	Remarks and references to Appendices
BRENTWOOD	1915 Dec 31	9-12	Sketches &c	
		2·3	Truthis lecture	
		4	Pay Parade	

Signature
OC 2/3 Bn 1st Aunts

2/3 Smd..... Appendix Summary.

Army Form C. 2118.

WAR DIARY
or
INTELLIGENCE SUMMARY.
(Erase heading not required.)

Instructions regarding War Diaries and Intelligence Summaries are contained in F.S. Regs., Part II. and the Staff Manual respectively. Title pages will be prepared in manuscript.

Place	Date	Hour	Summary of Events and Information	Remarks and references to Appendices
BRENTWOOD	Dec	1915	1. Continued tracing men int. lobellies for avwards. Kiv Collection, and treatment. Demolition forms. Due to force INGRAVE. the idea being that an encounter with the enemy had taken place in the neighbourhood of EAST HORDON. Lecture on back case from officer, on Why were brought in. II. S.Lt. GREAT WARLEY STREET. boundaries pat out. and collected. Enemy station found. and case lectured on. Lecture men & case from officer. III. LT. MAYES joined the unit before his name appeared in the Gazette. on Dec.23/5. IV. Sgt. S. WEALD COMMON. See idea was that an attack had been made on BRENTWOOD in that neighbourhood. Procedure as before. Lecture & Question on cases by officer. V. Patrol into dim SHENFIELD COMMON. collected and brought to HQ Where demoplation was carried out. Lecture given on cases by officer.	

B.M............
OC 2/3 Smd Ambulance.

Confidential

War Diary of
2/3rd South Midland Field Amb.ce
from Jan 1.c 1916 to. Jan 31.c 1916.

Army Form C. 2118.

WAR DIARY
or
INTELLIGENCE SUMMARY.
(Erase heading not required.)

Instructions regarding War Diaries and Intelligence Summaries are contained in F.S. Regs., Part II. and the Staff Manual respectively. Title pages will be prepared in manuscript.

Hour, Date, Place	Summary of Events and Information	Remarks and references to Appendices
1916		
BRENTWOOD. Jan 1.	Medical Inspection. General cleaning of kennels.	82
" 2.	Church parade for C.F.s. & nonconformist boxer	782
9–12 3	Route march.	782
2.4	Lecture and application of bandages & splints	
9.3 " 4	Field day. Simulation of Demonstration. Collection of wounded &c.	Appendix I. 182
9–12 " 5	Route march.	82
2.4	Lecture. First aid.	
9–12 " 6	Packing wagons & ambulances. Demonstration of powder cart.	782
2.4	Route march.	
9–12 " 7	[Lecture] general cleaning of kennels. Pay parade. Shah Benefactor arrived from SOUTHMINSTER.	782
9–12 " 8.	Medical Inspection. Short route march.	782

Army Form C. 2118.

WAR DIARY
or
INTELLIGENCE SUMMARY.
(Erase heading not required.)

Instructions regarding War Diaries and Intelligence Summaries are contained in F.S. Regs., Part II. and the Staff Manual respectively. Title pages will be prepared in manuscript.

1916	Hour, Date, Place		Summary of Events and Information	Remarks and references to Appendices
BRENTWOOD.		Jan. 9.	Church Parade. manœuvres.	
	10. a.m.	" 10	D. Coy. on Pte Drill. Gen.	92
			Capt. BOUCHER absent from here.	132
	9-12		Route march.	
	2-4		Demonstration of parade cart. Lecture on First aid.	
	9. a.m.	" 11	Promulgation of Sentence of DCM on Pte Drule.	52 Appendix II.
	9-3	"	Field day. Selection of wounded &c.	82
	9-12 2-3 3pp.	12	Packing & unpacking wagons. Lecture on ammunition & Sea ambs.	
	3-4		Short route march.	
	9-12	" 13	Route march.	52
	2-4	"	Packing & unloading wagons.	
	9-3	14	Brigade Field day. Capt. BOUCHER return from leave.	52 Appendix III.

Army Form C. 2118.

WAR DIARY
or
INTELLIGENCE SUMMARY.
(Erase heading not required.)

Instructions regarding War Diaries and Intelligence Summaries are contained in F.S. Regs., Part II and the Staff Manual respectively. Title pages will be prepared in manuscript.

Hour, Date, Place		Summary of Events and Information	Remarks and references to Appendices
BRENTWOOD	Jan 14	Lt. BRACHER gone on leave.	732
	" 15.	Medical Inspection. General cleaning of barrack.	732
	" 16	Church & nonconformist parade	732
9-12	" 17	Squad v Co. Drill.	
2.4.		Demonstration of gas attack. Washing apparatus &c. General fatigues.	732
		MAJOR CORFIELD. detailed for duty with R.F.A. SOUTHMINSTER.	Appendix IV
9.4.	18	Field day. Collection of wounded &c.	
9-12	19	Loading wagons &c.	732
2.4		Division of force to three sections. Lt. BROOKES on leave.	
9-12	" 20	Wagon drill.	732
2.4		Route march. Wounded convoy unloaded at station for COOMBE LODGE. 15 lying, 12 walking. Time 21 minutes.	

Army Form C. 2118.

WAR DIARY
or
INTELLIGENCE SUMMARY.
(Erase heading not required.)

Instructions regarding War Diaries and Intelligence Summaries are contained in F. S. Regs., Part II. and the Staff Manual respectively. Title pages will be prepared in manuscript.

Hour, Date, Place		Summary of Events and Information	Remarks and references to Appendices
BRENTWOOD.			
	Jan. 21.	Stitcher hire. CAPT. BOUCHER. & LT. MAYES re. DERBY	
	9.12.	LT. BRACHER. returned from leave. recruits WARLEY BARRACKS.	
	3.	Pay Parade.	
	" 22	General cleaning of kennels.	
	" 23	Church Parade. &c	
	" 24	Tent erection.	
9.12		Route march.	
2.4			
3-4		D.S.O. inspection of route cart.	
9.12	" 25	Packing & unboxing wagon.	
2.4		Route march.	
9.12	26	Demonstration of route cart.	
2.4		Route march.	

Army Form C. 2118.

WAR DIARY
or
INTELLIGENCE SUMMARY.
(Erase heading not required.)

Instructions regarding War Diaries and Intelligence Summaries are contained in F.S. Regs., Part II. and the Staff Manual respectively. Title pages will be prepared in manuscript.

Hour, Date, Place	Summary of Events and Information	Remarks and references to Appendices
BRENTWOOD. Jan 27.	Regimental Holiday.	Appendix V.
" 28		
9-12	Route march.	
2-4	Lecture: Boundaries & splint application	
4	Pay.	
" 29	General fatigue. Cleaning transport. Cooking lessons.	
9-12	CAPT BOUCHER & LT MAYES from DERBY recruits at WARLEY B. 732	
" 30	Church parade &c.	
	MAJOR CORFIELD returns off sick at WESTMINSTER	
" 31	Route march.	
9-12		
2-4	Lecture: Application of splints & practical demonstration. LT. BROOKE's return from leave	

B. Brown
Lt. Col.
O/C 3rd...
1st (2nd London) Division

Army Form C. 2118.

WAR DIARY
or
INTELLIGENCE SUMMARY.
(Erase heading not required.)

Instructions regarding War Diaries and Intelligence Summaries are contained in F.S. Regs., Part II and the Staff Manual respectively. Title pages will be prepared in manuscript.

Hour, Date, Place	Summary of Events and Information	Remarks and references to Appendices
Ref map. 108.05. 16/1	APPENDIX.	
	I. The guard idea was that an attack had been made; certain casualties had to be collected & brought to D.S.	S.D.
UPMINSTER COMMON.	II. The scheme found new details of D.S. Explained workings a/c practice at quick motoring & picking up. Site UPMINSTER COMMON.	S.D.
BILLERICAY	III. Defensive position at BILLERICAY. Pace granule .616. when details were given by Brig. 183 Inf Bde. D.S. formed at a farm N of second L in BILLERICAY. A.D.S. under MAJOR CORFIELD in BILLERICAY.	S.D.
UPMINSTER COMMON.	IV. Site UPMINSTER COMMON. D.S. in a barn of a farm. Wounded to be put out on common, collected & looked on. Squadron information. Motor cycle 1 one.	S.D.
INGRAVE.	V. Arrived into THORNDON PARK. D.S. formed at farm 1/2 NW of CROSS RDS. INGRAVE GREEN. Met and forage days. General operation orders.	S.D.

O/C 3rd Rfr. Amb.
61st (2d. Mid.) Division.

61st Division

2/Brd. S.M. Field Ambulance

April/16

May 1916

Army Form C. 2118.

WAR DIARY
or
INTELLIGENCE SUMMARY.
(Erase heading not required.)

Instructions regarding War Diaries and Intelligence Summaries are contained in F. S. Regs., Part II. and the Staff Manual respectively. Title pages will be prepared in manuscript.

Place	Date	Hour	Summary of Events and Information	Remarks and references to Appendices
PERHAM DOWN SALISBURY PLAIN	1.5.16		Route march and formation of Dressing Station	
	2.5.16		General routine.	
	3.5.16		Parades under section officers; bathing parades	
	4.5.16		General routine duties	
	5.5.16		Inspection by HIS MAJESTY THE KING at BULFORD FIELD	
	6.5.16		Medical Inspection and general routine. Scabies hospital opened at No 1 Camp Perham Down	
	7.5.16		Church parades	
	8.5.16		Field Amb takes part in Divisional Tactical Exercise	
	to		ditto	
	10.5.16		ditto	
	11.5.16		General routine & bathing parades	
	12.5.16		Parades under section officers. LT. MEENAN detailed for duty with 2/4 Bucks. Rgt.	
	13.5.16		Fatigues. Medical Inspection. LT. COL. ROGERS relinquishes command of Amb. and MAJOR CORFIELD assumes temporary command.	
	14.5.16		Church Parades.	
	15.5.16		Parades under section officers and lecture by O.C.	

Army Form C. 2118.

WAR DIARY
or
INTELLIGENCE SUMMARY.
(Erase heading not required.)

2/3 S.M. 2nd Cont. Vol I

Instructions regarding War Diaries and Intelligence Summaries are contained in F. S. Regs., Part II. and the Staff Manual respectively. Title pages will be prepared in manuscript.

Place	Date	Hour	Summary of Events and Information	Remarks and references to Appendices
PERHAM DOWN SALISBURY PLAIN	16.5.16		Field operations	P.h.
	7.5.16		Parades under section officers and bathing parades	P.h.
	18.5.16		General routine. A.D.M.S. lectures to Officers.	P.h.
	19.5.16		3rd Amb. takes part in Divisional Route March	P.h.
	20.5.16		Medical Inspection. Camp fatigues	P.h.
	21.5.16		Church parades	P.h.
	22.5.16		Fatigues; lectures by section officers	P.h.
	23.5.16		Fatigues. Camp chores preparatory to leaving same for overseas. Lectures by O.C. to N.C.O.'s.	P.h.
	24.5.16		Kit & Equipment inspection; loading wagons	P.h.
	25.5.16		Left TIDNORTH Station 10.20 A.M. arrived at SOUTHAMPTON 1 P.M. embarked 100 men C42 on H.M.S. CONNAUGHT remainder on H.M.S. ANGLO-CANADIAN	P.h.
	26.5.16		Arrived at HAVRE - marched to St. VIC rest camp No 2.	P.h.
	27.5.16		Entrained at HAVRE.	P.h.
	28.5.16		Travelling all day till 5 p.m. - Detrained at BURGUETTE - marched to BUSNES	P.h.
	29.5.16		General duties	P.h.
	30.5.16		General duties	P.h.
	31.5.16		Marched from BUSNES to ROBECQ - Took over Divisional Baths & Dressing Station.	P.h.

63rd Division

2/3 S.M. Field Ambulance

June 1916

Army Form C. 2118.

WAR DIARY
or
INTELLIGENCE SUMMARY.
(Erase heading not required.)

Instructions regarding War Diaries and Intelligence Summaries are contained in F. S. Regs., Part II. and the Staff Manual respectively. Title pages will be prepared in manuscript.

Place	Date	Hour	Summary of Events and Information	Remarks and references to Appendices
LA GORGUE	22.6.16		A.D.M.S. visited LA FLINQUE and 2 aid Posts. MAJOR CORFIELD returned to H.Qtrs and CAPT. WOOD to LA FLINQUE. REV. PERCY (Wesleyan) attached to Unit.	O/C
	23.6.16		Visited Divisional Baths re clothing etc.	19 O/C
	24.6.16		H.Qrs Ambulance inspected by D.D.M.S. XI Army Corps accompanied by A.D.M.S. Sox. Div. Satisfaction expressed.	29 O/C 50 O/C
	25.6.16		Hospital Duties. Gen. Routine	35 O/C
	26.6.16		REV. O'KELLY (R.C.) attached to Unit. CAPT. BOUCHER proceeded to GREEN BARN to replace LT. MEENAN who returned to H.Qrs.	35 O/C
	27.6.16		CAPT. FISHER replaced by LT. O'MEARA at GREEN BARN.	21 O/C
	28.6.16		MAJOR CORFIELD proceeded to GREEN BARN replacing LT. O'MEARA. CAPT. NIXON returned to H.Qrs from LA FLINQUE	70 O/C
	29.6.16		O.C. proceeded to LA FLINQUE and GREEN BARN thence to Hut hut at CROIX BARBEE. MAJOR CORFIELD, sick, returned to H.Qtrs; replaced by CAPT. FISHER.	51 O/C
	30.6.16		Heavy bombardment during night of June 29th-30th. CAPT. BOUCHER returned to H.Qrs from GREEN BARN: replaced by LT. MEENAN. G.O.C. visited hospital. Satisfaction again expressed.	80 O/C

O. Moore Lieut Col
2/3 Sth Fd Amb

Confidential

War Diary
of
2/1 3rd Field Ambulance
6th Division
July 1916.

Vol 3
South Midland
Volume 3

COMMITTEE FOR THE
MEDICAL HISTORY OF THE WAR
Date 13 SEP. 1916

WAR DIARY
INTELLIGENCE SUMMARY

Army Form C. 2118.

2/3 S.M. Fld Amb

Place	Date	Hour	Summary of Events and Information	Remarks and references to Appendices
LA GORGUE	1.7.16		Routine duties. Expedition of Ambulance Kg.s by D.A.D.M.S. X1th Corps. Enquiries were made if his staff several running orders should be withdrawn from the Advanced Dressing Station & hospitals to the hospital at this place. I considered that many orderlies were quite usefully employed at their duties at the Advanced Dressing Station & Sudan was relieved by C Section at GREEN BARN (A.D.S.) and Lt MEENAN was replaced by Capt BOUCHER.	Plu.
	2.7.16		Early in the morning was sent for by the A.D.M.S. He informed me that the enemy were attacking and that heavy casualties were expected and ordered me to send up 2 horsed waggons and all available cars. This order was rapidly carried out, the men having nearly all arrived & the line by the Ambulance cars, Capt. NIXON and Lieut MEENAN proceeding in charge. This procedure seemed to me to be incorrect as my own Advanced	Plu.

Place	Date	Hour	Summary of Events and Information	Remarks and references to Appendices
LA GORGUE	2.7.16		Dressing Station at LA FLINGUE (Map 36. M.27.d.5.3) and GREEN BARN (Map 36. M.10.c.5.2) were well staffed in every respect and had ample means of communication with one, and I should have received advice from the advanced Officers in charge of these Dressing Stations. It they had been unable to deal with the casualties and required assistance. As no such advice was received, it was found that no assistance whatever was required at LA FLINGUE and on proceeding to GREEN BARN some of the men were sent up to the trenches & were of some little assistance, but the greater number were left at the Dressing Station & the O.C. there (Capt BOUCHER) reported to me that they had only been in the way. The total number of wounded admitted was 55, which was slightly above the average. I should suggest that in any case our stretcher bearers sent up to the	Ph.

WAR DIARY or INTELLIGENCE SUMMARY

Place	Date	Hour	Summary of Events and Information	Remarks and references to Appendices
LA GORGUE.	2.7.16		Advanced Dressing Station without a request for assistance from the Medical Officer in charge of these Stations. I was on duty at H.Qs with Capn Copwell and we received of all night but were not told. Se men reported the Indians they were called upon for entirely surprising and took the G.O.C. 61st Div. and the 2 F.Hs. by surprise. He appeared to the arrangements made for dealing with the casualties.	Ph.
"	3.7.16		Quin. The 24 hours previous to 9am this morning 5 - 3 wounded were admitted and a total of 78 wounded evacuated to the Casualty Clearing Station MERVILLE (Ref: 36 A.K.29.d.9.1.) Richie Durkie.	Ph.
	4.7.16		Indian Hospitalworker	Ph.
	5.7.16		Indianworker. About midday lst there was a Gas Alarm. The guard turned out + warned all billets warning the	Ph.

Place	Date	Hour	Summary of Events and Information	Remarks and references to Appendices
LA GORGUE	5.7.16		occupants. All ranks had been instructed as soon as gatherers in the alert position as this had been expected. No gas was noticed here and at the end of an hour one man was ordered from each billet to remain awake - the remainder allowed to sleep. At the end of the 2nd hour the guard was changed until Reveille woke. The Bug. 1st Army visited GREEN BARN Dressing Station and inspected it. He expressed his satisfaction with arrangements made for dealing with cases.	Ply.
"	6.7.16		Instructions were received from the A.D.M.S. to hand over the Dressing Station at LA FLINQUE to the 2/1st S.M. Fd. Ambce. The instructions were received at 4 p.m. and all personnel equipment were at work at my Headquarters at 9 p.m., the relief having been effected. Further instructions were received from A.D.M.S for an Ambulance to take over up another position at	Ply.

Army Form C. 2118.

WAR DIARY
or
INTELLIGENCE SUMMARY.
(Erase heading not required.)

Place	Date	Hour	Summary of Events and Information	Remarks and references to Appendices
LA GORGUE	6-7-16		VIELLE CHAPELLE (Bethune Cambrai Sheet R.34.a.6.9.) All subsequent map references will be from the BETHUNE CAMBRAI Sheet. I carefully proceeded to VIELLE CHAPELLE to make arrangements with the O.C. 132nd Fd. Ambce. for the relief.	Plan
"	7-7-16		According at 6.30 am. Capt BOUCHER, Capt WOOB & Lieut MEENAN proceeded with the main body of the Ambulance to VIEUX CHAPELLE and took over the headquarters. Capt WOOB, Lt MEENAN & 40 men then marched to ST VAAST (M.32.d.5.3.) and took over the Dressing Station there and the Aid Posts at PLUM ST (S.10.a.d.3) and FACTORY CORNER (S.9.d.2.e.). Also the hut at RICHEBOURG ST VAAST (S.2.C.3.10.) and a Collecting Post at KING GEORGE's POST (X.5.d.5.2) were taken over & staffed by Capt WOOB. The 20 cars I had remaining at LA GORGUE were transferred to the V.A.S. Sn Fd Ambce, and at 10am I went to VIELLE CHAPELLE with Major CORFIELD, Lt. BROOKES and the remainder of the Ambulance. The unit was carried out exploring and exploiting	Plan

Place	Date	Hour	Summary of Events and Information	Remarks and references to Appendices
VIELLE CHAPELLE	7.7.16	12 noon	Reached VIELLE CHAPELLE & found my Headquarters. Some difficulty was experienced as regards transport, as it became essential either a Hospital is fixed, for any length of time, to collect extra equipment and on moving there is insufficient transport to move this. In the event of a move to a distance this would of course be kept behind. The horse equipment being rather a small bulky body of a Corporal & four men was sent to ZELOBES (R.26.d.16.4.) taking over this station from the 133rd Field Amb. and at 2 p.m. Capt FISHER took over with this Dressing Station with 20 men. At 2 p.m. the baths at VIELLE CHAPELLE were opened & that day 700 men of the 1st Camb. were bathed & supplied with clean underclothing.	Plv
"	8.7.16		Major CORFIELD had instructions to proceed to 2011 C.C.S. at DOULLENS to take up the duties of Anaesthetist. I visited the A.D.S.'s & posts and	Plv

WAR DIARY
INTELLIGENCE SUMMARY

Army Form C. 2118.

Place	Date	Hour	Summary of Events and Information	Remarks and references to Appendices
VIELLE CHAPELLE	8.7.16		was not satisfied as to the utility of ST VAAST as an Advanced Dressing Station. The dugouts and general accommodation for wounded was satisfactory, but the ground was also used as an R.E. dump and at the any time might be severely shelled. I decided to make it a collecting Post and made arrangements accordingly.	Ply
"	9.7.16		Visits of inspection were made by the 99th.S. XIth Corps, A.D.M.S. 2nd. F.A. & A.D.M.S. 61st Division and expedition was expressed. Lt. O'MEARA was detailed to take over duties of M.O. to the 3rd Glynmeu. The following letter was sent to the ADMS reporting on the arrangements made.	Ply
"	10.7.16		So ADMS. The medical arrangement in this area have now been completed and a report is forwarded for your information. The Headquarters of the 3rd Glynd Ambce is at VIELLE CHAPELLE (R.34.a.8.9.) There is an Advanced Dressing Station at	Ply

WAR DIARY or INTELLIGENCE SUMMARY.

Army Form C. 2118.

Place	Date	Hour	Summary of Events and Information	Remarks and references to Appendices
VIEILLE CHAPELLE	10.7.16		GREEN BARN (M.27.d.5.2.) and another Dressing Station at ZELOBES (R.21.d.5.2.) Collecting Posts have been established at ST. VAAST (M.32.d.7.4.) and KING GEORGE'S POST (X.5.d.5.2.) These two are staffed by a R.A.M.C. N.C.O. and 6 men and a Motor Ambulance is available at each. The Regimental Aid Posts are:—	
			(1) EBENEZER FARM (M.34.b.5.9.)	Route of evacuation
			(2) MOGG'S HOLE (M.35.b.5.6.)	By Tramway to Green Barn
			(3) STIRLING CASTLE (S.4.d.f.10.)	By road to Green Barn or Tramway to St Vaast
			(4) PLUM ST (S.10.a.8.3.)	By Tramway to St Vaast
			(5) FACTORY CORNER (S.9.d.2.8.)	By road to St Vaast
			(6) TUBE STATION (S.21.d.6.8.) (approached from own)	So 13th Field Ambulance
			(7) PATH HOUSE (S.14.c.5.3.)	By Tramway to King George's Post
			(8) SLOANE SQUARE (X.11.c.2.2.)	By road to King George's Post.
			Cases at St Vaast are evacuated by Erskine Ambulance	

WAR DIARY or INTELLIGENCE SUMMARY

Army Form C. 2118.

Place	Date	Hour	Summary of Events and Information	Remarks and references to Appendices
VIEILLE CHAPELLE	15.7.16		Field Ambulance ST VAAST, KING GEORGE'S POST, and RICHEBOURG ST VAAST. The relief was carried out without any trouble and at 2 p.m. we moved off to LA GORGUE.	Ats
" "	"	4 pm	Arrived at LA GORGUE.	Ats Ats
LA GORGUE	16.7.16		Received instructions to open our headquarters for the reception of cases, and also the fit up the Divisional Theatre for the reception of walking + sitting cases. Capt MOORE & Lt MEENAN with 8 or others went to Capt NIXON. Capt MOORE & Lt MEENAN with 8 or others went to camp at the latter. An arrangement is to was drawn up to admit for two weeks only. 36 stretcher bearers arrived from 2/1st S. Ml. field Amb. Bearer work.	
"	17.7.16		Capt MOORE, Capt WILKINSON & bearers returned to 2/1st field ambce. Lt McMINN taken on the strength from 2/1st W.S. Ml. field ambce who expressed approval of arrangements made for the reception of cases.	Ats Ats
"	18.7.16			
"	19.7.16		Capt MOORE & 36 men from 2/1st S. Ml. fld Ambce joined at 9.30 am to assist	Ats

WAR DIARY
INTELLIGENCE SUMMARY

Army Form C. 2118.

Place	Date	Hour	Summary of Events and Information	Remarks and references to Appendices
LA GORGUE	19.7.16		On heavy casualties were expected. Two cars were also sent to no Lieut ALEXANDER & Lieut BLACKMORE of the 93rd F. Amb. were also attached for duty. Capt NIXON, Capt MOORE & Lieut BLACKMORE did duty at the Divisional Rest Station. Myself, Capt BOUCHER, Lt McMINN & Lt ALEXANDER were on duty at the two dressing stations. Casualties commenced arriving at 6 p.m. in response to requests from Major MACKIE, Capt WOOD, Capt FISHER & Lt MEENAN with 90 stretcher bearers were sent up to LAVENTIE Dressing Station (M.4.a.8.10.) to assist, Lt MEENAN going forward to RED HOUSE (M.12.a.1.10.). All available cars and three Ambulances were sent up to LAVENTIE. During the night a total of 198 lying cases were evacuated from here to the C.C.S. at MERVILLE and 504 sitting cases were dealt with at the Divisional Shelter. During the day visits were paid by the 9th K.G., 1st Army, 2nd Corps & 2nd Cav. Div. X.1st Corps.	8th
"	20/7/16		All cases were cleared by 9 am and after this there was only the normal routine to be carried out. All	8th

WAR DIARY or INTELLIGENCE SUMMARY

Place	Date	Hour	Summary of Events and Information	Remarks and references to Appendices
A 9.7.40E	24/7/16		All detachments of the A.D.S. at LAVENTIE returned, the bearers being absolutely exhausted. The wounded were all dealt with speedily and without a hitch and the work done was very creditable. Points for notice were:— (1) On arrival at the Regtl Aid Post, no stretcher bearers did not know their way into the front line trenches and there was no one to tell them the way, with the consequence that much energy was wasted in wandering about. (2) Also it would seem to me to be advisable to send allowable stretcher bearers up early in the engagement. They could not all be needed at once & then would have been opportunity in the evacuating trenches. The bringing in of large numbers from the A.D.S. would cause congestion there. Liaison has made the following statement on the arrangements from his pair of members the Regimental Aid Post at RED HOUSE.	Sks.

Army Form C. 2118.

WAR DIARY
or
INTELLIGENCE SUMMARY.
(Erase heading not required.)

Place	Date	Hour	Summary of Events and Information	Remarks and references to Appendices
LA GORGUE	28/7/16		"Being upon the trenches on the right of the Divisional fighting I devoted a few minutes to which may be of interest - the time was up in between 3 am & 5 am. (1) The wheeled stretcher could have been used to greater advantage. This will be rendered by a little diagram. The wheeled stretcher were kept at A with the wounded that the stretcher bearers had to carry stretchers along the road from C & B to A, a distance of about one mile - they could have been brought up to C and B. [sketch: arrow "To Laventie A.D.S.", "RED HOUSE", "Julio Lodge", points A, B, C, "Breastwork trench", "Railway", "Rifleman's Avenue"] (2) There was very little use made of the railway line and no use made of the trollies. The line was broken only in two places and a little ingenuity could have	Sk.

Place	Date	Hour	Summary of Events and Information	Remarks and references to Appendices
GRGOE	2/7/16		overrunts this. The Divn asked by using the railway's about half that that required to come through the trenches.	the

(3) The Regimental Sketches teams had no system of whatever, it showed that they were quite fatigued. I many sketches had no oriings.

(4)

(5) I should suggest a reliable NCO to be detailed to patrol the roads, trenches or railway whereabouts it would be to have the roads & the best trenches to go up and down, and to see that the men were doing their duty.

(6) The fact of the line to be covered should be divided into different parts and a certain number of Stretcher Bearers told off to each part, this would avoid too many going to one part of the line and none to the other, as was the case with one part of the line I visited. Again the bearers for the most part forgot that there were stretches of trenches to

WAR DIARY
or
INTELLIGENCE SUMMARY.

(Erase heading not required.)

Army Form C. 2118.

Place	Date	Hour	Summary of Events and Information	Remarks and references to Appendices
LA GORGUE	29/7/16			Rlm

These observations indicate direction in which improvement can be made, and I am making enquiries with a view to finishing everything in the future. We found that with quite a small staff at work at the main dressing station we could of well dispose of the work. Any stretcher cases came here, from in a car; two were placed in an dressing room + two in the other. These were attended to and given antiketanic serum and were then taken to the evacuating room. The details were taken by the clerks and transfer forms made out, entries made in the ADP book and the A.36 kept up to date. This seemed to me an

(Signed) Lieut Newman
3rd Fd. Amb.

Place	Date	Hour	Summary of Events and Information	Remarks and references to Appendices
LA GORGUE	20.7.16		improved method for a rush. The doctors were not kept working while patients were not, and the patients were not moved while they had been dressed, had admits & made comfortable. By means of carbon paper duplicates on the transfer form were also made in all of the fresh patients in A&D books and the A.&.36.: This method considerably expedited the handling of cases. Ambulances from cars were on the transfer form. They were placed in a motor ambulance Convoy car & taken to the C.C.S. The Convoy was a continuous service. We were at work here continuing from 6 p.m. 19 to 6 a.m. 20 and up to this moment. Rainier ever since but though, had at no time more than 6 cases waiting for attention or transfer when I think speaks for the facility of the arrangements. Kits were put by the 2nd S. Corps and 28rd Div.	Ske—

Army Form C. 2118.

WAR DIARY
or
~~INTELLIGENCE SUMMARY.~~
(Erase heading not required.)

Instructions regarding War Diaries and Intelligence Summaries are contained in F. S. Regs., Part II. and the Staff Manual respectively. Title pages will be prepared in manuscript.

Place	Date	Hour	Summary of Events and Information	Remarks and references to Appendices
LA GORGUE	20.7.16	5 p.m.	Capt MOORE had order to rejoin his unit with the section which had been attached to us. He left for MERVILLE at 6 p.m.	The
"	21.7.16		Lt. ALEXANDER & BLACKMORE returned to the 93rd Field Amb. Divisional theatre closed down. Capt NIXON returning with his section to Headquarters.	The
"	22.7.16		Capt. FISHER detailed for duty with 307 Brigade R.F.A. vice Capt. MAYES who proceeds to Div. A.D.S. for duty General routine.	The
"	23.7.16		LA FLINGUE dressing station taken over by Capts NIXON, WOOD, Lt M'MINN and 40 men	The
"	24.7.16		Raided LA FLINGUE. This lead we held this station. The Artillery have feared a bursar in the same field. This is unfortunate as it is certain to attract attention & render the station untenable. Apparently there is nothing to prevent Artillery placing guns in any position they fancy, at the	The

Army Form C. 2118.

WAR DIARY
or
INTELLIGENCE SUMMARY.
(Erase heading not required.)

Instructions regarding War Diaries and Intelligence Summaries are contained in F. S. Regs., Part II. and the Staff Manual respectively. Title pages will be prepared in manuscript.

Place	Date	Hour	Summary of Events and Information	Remarks and references to Appendices
La GORGUE	25.7.16		Some time was considered might be made for dressing station as it is not always easy to find suitable billets for them.	Plu
"	26.7.16		General routine work.	Plu
"	27.7.16		Enquiries of all sorts were gone through with a view	Plu
"			to having all deficiencies replaced.	Plu
"	28.7.16		Ordered Hospital work. Any work.	Plu
"	29.7.16		General work. Visit by A.D.M.S.	Plu
"	30.7.16		Capt BOUCHER visited the A.D.S. at LA FLINGUE.	Plu
"	31.7.16		General routine work.	Plu

R. Huxey, Major. R.A.M.C.
O/C 3rd Fld Amb

Aug. 1916.

Vol 4

War Diary

2/3 S. m. Field Ambulance

Volume 4.

WAR DIARY
or
INTELLIGENCE SUMMARY.

Army Form C. 2118.

Place	Date	Hour	Summary of Events and Information	Remarks and references to Appendices
LA GORGUE	1.8.16	12 noon	Routine work. Lt McMINN relieved Lt McMINN at LA FLINQUE. Kondulcia carried out.	—
"	2.8.16	"	Routine work.	—
"	3.8.16	"	Lt HANSON relieves Lt MEENAN at LA FLINQUE.	—
"	4.8.16	"	Lt MEENAN is detailed for duty as M.O. to the 2/6th glost. Regt., replacing Lt O'MEARA who rejoins the unit. Wadsworth.	—
"	5.8.16	"	General hospital nature. Spots were held by the unit and were entirely successful. Wadsworth.	—
"	6.8.16	"	Church parades. Wadsworth.	—
"	7.8.16	"	Capt. MAYES having transferred to the R.E.'s was struck off the strength. N.C.O.'s & men at LA FLINQUE, PONT DU HEM baths & PONT RIQUEUL baths were visited and relieved by a detachment from LA GORGUE. Lt McMINN replaced Capt NIXON.	—
"	8.8.16	"	Lt P. NASE transferred & attached for duty. Wadsworth.	—
"	9.8.16	"		—
"	10.8.16	"	Visited LA FLINQUE & found everything in order. Visit from A.D.M.S.	—

WAR DIARY
or
INTELLIGENCE SUMMARY.

(Erase heading not required.)

Army Form C. 2118.

Place	Date	Hour	Summary of Events and Information	Remarks and references to Appendices
LA GORGUE	11.8.16	2 p.m.	A N.C.O. was sent for a course at the Gas Defence School. Routine indoor outdoor work.	Ph.
"	12.8.16	"	Lt. NASE replaces Lt. HANCON at LA FLINGUE. Visit from D.D.M.S. XI Corps.	Ph.
"	13.8.16	"	Church parades and routine work	Ph.
"	14.8.16	"	Capt FISHER having transferred to the Highland C.C.S. w'shall off the strength. Carried out an inspection of billets whatever was satisfactory condition. Attended a lecture on 'gas gangrene' by Col. C. WALLACE R.A.M.C. Lieut. H.G. CARLISLE was temporarily attached for duty.	Ph.
"	15.8.16	"	Visited Divisional workshop. Inspection of transport wagons, animals & harness. Routine work.	Ph.
"	16.8.16	"	Routine indoor outdoor work. Visit to LA FLINGUE.	Ph.
"	17.8.16	"	General routine. Capt BOUCHER exchanged with Capt ANDERSON of No. 2. Ind Ambulance Convoy. Inspected by A.D.M.S. Lt Col A.E. GREENBERN from 93rd Field Ambulance	Ph.
"	18.8.16	"		Ph.

WAR DIARY or INTELLIGENCE SUMMARY

Army Form C. 2118.

Place	Date	Hour	Summary of Events and Information	Remarks and references to Appendices
LAGORGE	8.8.16	noon	GREEN BARN Rehearsal for from 93rd Field Ambulance of 31 N.C.O.'s and men under Capt ANDERSON, Lt O'MEARA and Lt HANSON	Phr
"	19.8.16		Routine work. Escort of T.U. men taken over by Lt Anderson	Phr
"	20.8.16		2 several N.C.O. detailed for training at the Divisional Gas School	Phr
"	21.8.16		Visited LA FLINGUE & GREEN BARN. General work	Phr / Phr
"	22.8.16		Capt WOOD returned from LA FLINGUE. Pickets at Headquarters being replaced by Lt HANSON from GREEN BARN.	—
"	23.8.16		Lt NASE returned from LA FLINGUE to Headquarters and to detailed to attend a course at Chysoelsarney with 2 N.C.O's	Phr / Phr / Phr / Phr
"	24.8.16		Lecture by Capt Dubuisson	
"	25.8.16		Routine work. Visit from Capt PARKINSON Sanitary Officer 1st Army. Suggestions received by him above being carried out. Lt SKEEN arrived and was attached for duty	
"	26.8.16		Lt H.Q. CARLISLE dispatched to BOULOGNE for autopsy instruction from D.D.M.S. Base	Phr
"	27.8.16		GREEN BARN personnel on the 93rd Fd Amb. Church parades. Routine work	Phr

Army Form C. 2118.

WAR DIARY
or
INTELLIGENCE SUMMARY.
(Erase heading not required.)

Instructions regarding War Diaries and Intelligence Summaries are contained in F. S. Regs., Part II. and the Staff Manual respectively. Title pages will be prepared in manuscript.

Place	Date	Hour	Summary of Events and Information	Remarks and references to Appendices
LAGORGUE	28.8.16		Return of LAFINGUE relieved by section from Headquarters. Capt ANDERSON, Lt SKEEN and Lt NASE being the officers in charge. R.C.O.'s run at the PONT-DU-HEM & PONT RIQUEUL both are replied by T.V. men.	Ph.
" "	29.8.16		10 pairs of draft horses & harness sent to No 3 40 A.S.C. Armentières	Ph.
" "	30.8.16		Capt NIXON 10 transferred to No 36 C.C.S. for entry. Routine work. Visit from A.D.M.S. Lt McMINN was unread to No 2 Leading the C.C.S. expenditure	Ph. Ph.
" "	31.8.16		For appendices. Lecture by Capt Gibson — Nursing in lungs at the C.C.S. in its relation to Field Ambulance work. Routine work	Ph. Ph.

O. Mason Major
2/3 S.W. Fd Amb.
1st Div

61st Div.

Sept. 1916

Confidential

Vol 5

War Diary.
2/3rd Field Ambulance. 61st Div.
September 1916
Volume 5.

COMMITTEE FOR THE
MEDICAL HISTORY OF THE WAR
Date 26 OCT. 1916

WAR DIARY or INTELLIGENCE SUMMARY.

Army Form C. 2118.

(Erase heading not required.)

Instructions regarding War Diaries and Intelligence Summaries are contained in F. S. Regs., Part II. and the Staff Manual respectively. Title pages will be prepared in manuscript.

Place	Date	Hour	Summary of Events and Information	Remarks and references to Appendices
LA GORGUE. 36A. L.35.b.9.9.	1.IX.16		Ambulance inspected by the D.D.M.S. XI Corps. Lashaparty. Three N.C.O.'s detailed for instruction in hive deterram and destruction.	—
	2.IX.16		Routine work. Lieut NASE proceeded to LAFLINQUE (36 — M.10.c.8.1.) for duty.	—
	3.IX.16		Visited by the A.D.M.S. 61st Div. Lieut. MILLS R.M. Rahn on the strength on reporting from three days duty. Routine work.	—
	4.IX.16		—	—
	5.IX.16		Inspection of the Ambulance by the G.O.C. 61st Division who expressed his approval of our work.	—
	6.9.16		Our V.C.O. detailed for a course of instruction at the Gas School. One reinforcement arrived transferred from 1/3 W.L. R.A.M.C.	—
	7.9.16		A N.C.O. & two men detailed for duty at Corps Laundry.	—
	8.9.16		Visit from A.D.M.S. Routine work. Capt EVANS taken on the strength.	—
	9.9.16		2 N.C.O.'s detailed for instruction in disinfectin.	—

WAR DIARY or INTELLIGENCE SUMMARY.

Army Form C. 2118.

Place	Date	Hour	Summary of Events and Information	Remarks and references to Appendices
LA GORGUE	10/9/16		Conference of O.C. Divisions at the A.D.S.S.'s with reference to the attachment of them to the charge of the Divisional supervision of areas in the Division. Capt WOOD detailed to inspect the explosives (1.21.a.2.7.) EBENEZER FARM (M.27.d.7.3.) & PONT DUHEM with reference	S/L
	11/9/16		to evening party of erraters Inverded visited PONT DUHEM both with D.A.D.S. & Capt WOOD and suggested alteration.	S/L
	12/9/16		Routine work. Inspected the horse standings being erected by us for the winter.	S/L
	13/9/16		Two reinforcements arrived from the base.	S/L
	14/9/16		Visited LA FLINQUE (36 M.10.C.8.1.) & PONT DUHEM Depot. Lieut SKEEN detailed for duty with the S.M.R.E's. Capt EVANS placed in charge of the PONT DUHEM area as Sanitary Officer	S/L S/L S/L S/L

WAR DIARY
or
INTELLIGENCE SUMMARY.

Army Form C. 2118.

Place	Date	Hour	Summary of Events and Information	Remarks and references to Appendices
LA GORGUE	15.9.16		Routine work. Inspected a well which has been sunk for the supply of water for ablution. Water supply good and satisfactory. Kit inspection - coats to all billets.	OCh
	16.9.16		Commndg Officers inspection. Visit of inspection by the D.D.S. 1st Army, who expressed his satisfaction with the work of the ambulance in all its departments. He also visited the A.D.S. at LA FLINQUE & remarked on the improvements carried out since his previous visit.	OCh
	17.9.16		Lieut HANSON detached transferred to the 97" Field Ambulance Lieut O'MEARA and Lieut NASE proceeded to the A.D.S. for duty. GREEN BARN during absence taken over by us from the 93rd Field Ambulance. Routine work.	OCh
	18.9.16		Routine work.	OCh
	19.9.16		Kit to A.D.S. - Routine work.	OCh

Army Form C. 2118.

WAR DIARY
or
INTELLIGENCE SUMMARY.
(Erase heading not required.)

Place	Date	Hour	Summary of Events and Information	Remarks and references to Appendices
LA GORGUE	20.9.16		Visited all billets occupied by the Ambulance. Found them in a clean & satisfactory condition.	Ph/
	21.9.16		Ruthinen-ha. Inspection of kits for deficiencies.	Ph/
	22.9.16		Lecture to Officers, N.C.O.'s & men on "Gas" by Sergt. Lewin who had returned from a course of instruction at the Gas School. Proceeded on leave. Capt. Wood being placed temporarily in command.	Ph/ Ph/
	23.9.16		Ruthine work.	Ph/
	24.9.16		Inspection of A.D.S.'s by Capt Wood.	Ph/
	25.9.16		General hospital routine.	Ph/
	26.9.16		Ruthenework. 3 Reinforcements arrived.	Ph/
	27.9.16		Routine work.	Ph/
	28.9.16		Inspection of billets by Capt Wood.	Ph/
	29.9.16		Lieut O'MEARA detached for duty with the 2/1st Bucks Batt'n.	
	30.9.16		Inspection by the A.A. & Q.M.G. 61st Div. Ruthenework. Inspection of all T.U. men. Ruthenework.	Ph/

P. Moxey. Surgn. Maur??
O/C 2/3rd S.M. Field Ambulance.

Oct 1916 140/188

61st Division

2/3 S.M. Field Ambulance

COMMITTEE FOR THE
MEDICAL HISTORY OF THE WAR
Date -2 DEC. 1915

Army Form C. 2118.

2/3 SM ant
Vol 6

WAR DIARY
or
INTELLIGENCE SUMMARY.
(Erase heading not required.)

Place	Date	Hour	Summary of Events and Information	Remarks and references to Appendices
LA GORGUE	Sept 1916		Routine work	Plu
"	2.10.16		MAJOR MOXEY returned from leave. Capt ANDERSON, Lieut O'MEARA and Lieut SKEEN were transferred to the 31st Division on instructions received from the A.D.M.S.	Plu
"	3.10.16		Visit was unpaid by the G.O.C. 61st Division accompanied by an officer from the Divisional Hospital Staff. Visit of inspection by the D.M.S. 1st Army, who expressed his satisfaction with the work and appearance of the Ambulance.	Plu
"	4.10.16		Capt WOOD proceeded on leave. Inspected LA FLINGUE and GREEN BARN dressing stations. Routine work. Lecture by Major FRANKAU on War Surgery.	Plu
"	5.10.16			Plu
"	6.10.16		Lieut NASE and Lieut SEVIER detached to attend a course of Instruction to Schools of Instruction.	Plu
"	7.10.16			Plu
"	8.10.16		Routine work. Anderson (D Shampson) proceeded on leave.	Plu
"	9.10.16		Visit to Divisional workshops and inspection of lorries approved.	Plu
"	10.10.16		Visit to A.D.M.S.	Plu

Army Form C. 2118.

WAR DIARY
or
INTELLIGENCE SUMMARY.
(Erase heading not required.)

Place	Date	Hour	Summary of Events and Information	Remarks and references to Appendices
LA GORGUE	11.10.16		Lieut MILLS proceeded on leave. Capt EVANS took charge at LA FLINQUE. Lieut EVANS returns to LA GORGUE not being admitted into hospital. Lieut O'BOYLE from the 3rd Division reported here unless returning from A.D.M.S.	Ph.
"	12.10.16		Lieut O'BOYLE transferred to the 8th Division on returning from A.D.M.S.	Ph.
"	13.10.16		Routineworks	
"	14.10.16		Capt WOOD returned from leave. Kit inspection in different billets	Ph.
"	15.10.16		Lieut NASE instructed to report for duty with the 7th R. Warwick. Routineworks.	Ph.
"	16.10.16		Carried at GREEN BARN A.D.S. relieved by an equal number from Headquarters.	Ph.
"	17.10.16		Lieut NASE returned to the Ambulance for duty and posted to GREEN BARN.	Ph.
"	18.10.16		Routineworks	Ph.
"	19.10.16		Kit inspection with a view to supplying deficiencies and newclothing	Ph.

WAR DIARY
or
INTELLIGENCE SUMMARY.

(Erase heading not required.)

Army Form C. 2118.

Place	Date	Hour	Summary of Events and Information	Remarks and references to Appendices
LA GORGUE	19.10.16		Attended a conference at the A.D.M.S. office.	Ahn
"	20.10.16		Capt MARSHALL detailed for duty with the 1/2th Field Ambulance. Visit of inspection by A.D.M.S. who expressed his satisfaction at the appearance of the men and transport. Lt MILLS returned from leave. Kit inspection. Rechristened.	Ahn
"	21.10.16		Lieut MILLS returned from leave. Capt MARSHALL posted to the 2/2 N. Field Ambulance.	2hn Ahn
"	22.10.16		Inspection of M.T.s. Lorries in horse Ambulance wagons fitted with boxes for the purpose of carrying dressings &c. With the present arrangement it is impossible to pack anything in them lorries.	Ahn
"	23.10.16		Lt MILLS replaces Lieut NASE at GREEN BARN. L/Sergeant BRUNT returned from a month's leave in England.	
"	24.10.16		Lt MARRIOTT & Lieut BELLEW posted to this unit on being inspection of transport.	Ahn

WAR DIARY or INTELLIGENCE SUMMARY

Army Form C. 2118.

Place	Date	Hour	Summary of Events and Information	Remarks and references to Appendices
LA GORGUE	25.10.16		Major BREBNER & 2/1st London Field Ambce arrived as arranged about 10 h noon. Advance party.	O/C
"	26.10.16		Lieut JONES-EVANS handed over to the 2/1st Fd Ambce. Reports of billets. Parties from 2/1st London Fd Ambce arrived and took over the A.D.S. at LAFLINGUE & GREEN BARN, also detachments relieved returning to headquarters.	O/C
"	27.10.16		A small party from the relieving Ambce also took over charge of the hospital at LA GORGUE. All wagons packed ready for moving off.	O/C
"	28.10.16	8am	Marched to Chateau de Quesnoy, CHATEAU DE QUESNOY. (Map 36A. V.2.b.5.9.) via LESTREM, FOSSE, LE CORNET MALO, ROBECQ, L'ECLEM, arriving at 3.30 pm. The men were well done and only 6 men fell out.	O/C
LE CORNET MALO	29.10.16		Rearranged loading of wagons, so that all equipment necessary for upkeep of our A.D.S. is now contained in our limber carts.	O/C
"	30.10.16		Clean billets, baths, wagons, and general overhaul.	O/C
"	31.10.16		Routine work. Lieut LENNAN posted to the unit for duty.	O/C

Bluck, Major O.C.
O.C. 2/3 H. H. Fd Ambce.

140/249

Confidential

Vol 7

War Diary

19th F.M. Field Ambulance

61st Division

Period 1. 30. November 1916.

Valence 1.

Nov 916

COMMITTEE FOR THE
MEDICAL HISTORY OF THE WAR
Date -3 JAN. 1917

Army Form C. 2118.

WAR DIARY
or
INTELLIGENCE SUMMARY.
(Erase heading not required.)

Instructions regarding War Diaries and Intelligence Summaries are contained in F. S. Regs., Part II. and the Staff Manual respectively. Title pages will be prepared in manuscript.

Place	Date	Hour	Summary of Events and Information	Remarks and references to Appendices
RAIMBERT	1.11.16	5 p.m.	Field Ambulance marched from Chateau QUESNOY at 9 a.m. to RAIMBERT arriving there at 3 p.m.	Rpt.
ROCOURT	2.11.16	5 p.m.	At 8.30 left RAIMBERT & marched to ROCOURT arriving at 3.30 p.m.	Rpt.
QUESTREVILLE	3.11.16	5 p.m.	Marched from ROCOURT to QUESTREVILLE; moving off at 9.45 a.m. arriving 1 p.m. Roads were difficult and muddy and there was some trouble with the transport	Rpt.
"	4.11.16	12 noon	Remained for one days rest. Overhauled wagon equipment.	Rpt.
MAISNIL ST POL	5.11.16	5 p.m.	Left QUESTREVILLE at 9 a.m. & marched to MAISNIL ST POL arriving at 1.30 p.m.	Rpt.
BOFFLES	6.11.16	5 p.m.	Marched to BOFFLES arriving at 3 p.m. Lieut BELLEW reported sick & was evacuated to C.C.S.	Rpt.
"	7.11.16	12 noon	Overhauled equipment, under carts &c. Replaced damaged wheel by spares and greased wagon wheels. Major P. MOXEY appointed Lieut. Col whilst commanding a Field Ambulance dated from Aug 22nd 1916.	Rpt.
"	8.11.16	5 p.m.	Routine work.	Rpt.
"	9.11.16	5 p.m.	Shod mules march.	Rpt.
"	10.11.16	5 p.m.	Inspection of all gas helmets. Routine work.	Rpt.

Army Form C. 2118.

WAR DIARY
or
INTELLIGENCE SUMMARY.
(Erase heading not required.)

Instructions regarding War Diaries and Intelligence Summaries are contained in F. S. Regs., Part II. and the Staff Manual respectively. Title pages will be prepared in manuscript.

Place	Date	Hour	Summary of Events and Information	Remarks and references to Appendices
BOFFLES.	11.11.16	5pm	Lecture on Box Respirators by Lieut Levin. Routine work.	Ply
"	12.11.16	5pm	At 11 am. received instructions from A.D.M.S. for all bearers to parade uninitialed & march to FROHEN-LE-GRAND. They moved off at 12 noon under Lieuts MILLS, MARRIOTT & NASE, thence, from the last named place to HESAUVILLE. Here they were attached to the Royal Naval Division for work in the front line.	Ply.
"	13.11.16	5pm	Routine work.	Ply
"	14.11.16	5pm	General duties	Ply
LE MEILLARD	15.11.16	5pm	Entrained from Stn BOFFLES to LE MEILLARD	Ply.
LA HAIE FARM	16.11.16	5pm	Marched to LA HAIE FARM.	Ply
LA VICOGNE	17.11.16	5pm	Marched to LA VICOGNE	Ply
WARLOY.	18.11.16	5pm	Continued to march to WARLOY where we were billeted under canvas. Arrived 5pm.	Ply
			On all these marches the men have suffered considerably from the inability to get hot meals. A Field Ambulance possesses no Field cookers altho' it is larger than a company	

2353 Wt. W2544/1454 700,000 5/15 D. D. & L. A.D.S.S./Forms/C. 2118.

WAR DIARY
INTELLIGENCE SUMMARY

Army Form C. 2118.

Place	Date	Hour	Summary of Events and Information	Remarks and references to Appendices
WARLOY	19.11.16	5 p.m.	Infantry: It has only been possible to track those rations for the midday meal. As nearly our billets have not been possible to arrange the hot meal there we only have sufficient men to provide either a hot stew or tea, and it is found by experience that the men cannot do without the latter & therefore must forgo the former. This in my opinion is very unsatisfactory. Even after the end of the march it takes some two hours to prepare meals as kitchens have to be built, this let me when with a cooker the meal can be arranged for any time convenient. During the extreme cold weather I take this has undoubtedly affected the men's health.	Ely
MARTINSART	19.11.16	5 p.m.	Marched from WARLOY to MARTINSART	Ely
"	20.11.16	5 p.m.	Brown Section under Lieuts MILLS, MARRIOTT & NASE returned after their work with the Royal Naval Division.	Ely
"	21.11.16	5 p.m.		Ely
"	22.11.16	5 p.m.	A Section to debarks under Lieuts MILLS & MARRIOTT proceeded to Schwaben	Ely

WAR DIARY or INTELLIGENCE SUMMARY

Army Form C. 2118.

Place	Date	Hour	Summary of Events and Information	Remarks and references to Appendices
MARTINSART	22.11.16	5pm	Advanced posts at Danube handed over to the 59th Field Ambulance	Ph.
CABSTAND	23.11.16	5pm	Headquarters moved to CABSTAND. Lieut NASH & one private taken over Barley AVELUY POST. A NCO & 5 men take over the posts at BOUZINCOURT. The following posts are now held by us. (Map 57D) CABSTAND - W.10.C.6.3. AVELUY POST W.11.d.5-9. DONNET POST X.7.a.0.2. DANUBE TRENCH R.32.C.6.8. REGINA TRENCH GRAVEL PARK R.27.C.6.4. QUARRY POST R.33.6.2.3. OVILLERS REST HOUSE X.8.6.8.8. BOUZINCOURT MED. STORES. W.7.d.2.4. There are also on water duty with the Sanitary section at CRUCIFIX CORNER W.11.d.8.3. and W.11.d.1.7. OVILLERS RD X.8.C.3.5. BENNET ST X.8.6.1.5. DONNET POST X.7.C.5.5. THIEPVAL RD R.32.6.6.8. & R.32.C.6.8. AUTHIEVILLE WOOD X.1.d.9.9. & X.1.c.a.8.	Ph.
"	24.11.16	7pm	Lieut D.T. EVANS reported for duty. Medical Stores at BOUZINCOURT which had been taken over from the 59th Field Ambulance were handed over to OC No 20 M.A.C.	Ph.
"	25.11.16	5pm	Capt ROBSON reported for duty	Ph.
"	26.11.16	5pm	Private with Lieut NASH & 2 men to duty	Ph.
"	27.11.16	5pm	Lieut NASH standed for AVELUY POST to OC 2/1 S.M. Fd. Ambre & turned with party	Ph.

Army Form C. 2118.

WAR DIARY
or
INTELLIGENCE SUMMARY.
(Erase heading not required.)

Instructions regarding War Diaries and Intelligence Summaries are contained in F.S. Regs., Part II. and the Staff Manual respectively. Title pages will be prepared in manuscript.

Place	Date	Hour	Summary of Events and Information	Remarks and references to Appendices
CABSTAND	28.11.16	5 p.m.	to CABSTAND. A holding party of 1 NCO + 7 men sent to relieve guards at VARENNES (P.25.d.3.4) where we have been ordered to open a Divisional Rest Station. Lieut D.T. EVANS detailed as M.O. to 2/6 R. WARWICKS.	Ph
VARENNES	28.11.16	5 p.m.	Opened Headquarters at VARENNES. 2 Officers and 30 other ranks at CABSTAND to work the station there. Preparation of huts and kits for the reception of cases. Capt. CORNELIUS reported for duty.	Ph
"	29.11.16	5 p.m.	Lieut MARRIOTT detailed for duty with the 2/7 R. Warwicks during the absence of the M.O. on leave.	Ph
"	30.11.16	5 p.m.	Capt. ROBSON posted to DANUBE TRENCH, Capt. WOOD taking charge at CABSTAND	Ph

R. Covey Lt Col.
O.C. 2/3 F.S.h. Fld. Amb.

140/900 Confidence

War Diary
2/3 Field Ambulance
61st Div.
December 1916
Volume 8.

Dec 1916

COMMITTEE FOR THE
MEDICAL HISTORY OF THE WAR
Date 31 JAN. 1917

Vol 8

Army Form C. 2118.

WAR DIARY
or
INTELLIGENCE SUMMARY.

Army of ALBERT (COMBINED SHEET)

(Erase heading not required.)

Instructions regarding War Diaries and Intelligence Summaries are contained in F.S. Regs., Part II. and the Staff Manual respectively. Title pages will be prepared in manuscript.

Place	Date	Hour	Summary of Events and Information	Remarks and references to Appendices
VARENNES.	1.12.16		Capt. CORNELIUS R.A.M.C. (S.R.) taken on the strength. Five men detailed for duty at DANUBE TRENCH (R.32.c.6.8.) A Sergeant and	Ph
"	2.12.16		Lieut MARRIOTT detailed for temporary duty with 2/7 N. Humberland Fus. Two additional cars attached to us from the 2/wos.R. Field Amb.	Ph
"	3.12.16		Capt. CORNELIUS up lines Lieut NASE at DANUBE TRENCH (R.32.c.6.8.)	Ph
"	4.12.16		Routine work.	Ph
"	5.12.16		Col. YOUNG A.D.M.S. 61st Divn arrived and transferred to us Y Cavalry Chaing Stn. VARENNES (P-25.d.3.0.) visited CABSTAND (W.10.c.5.3.)	Ph
"	6.12.16		T. WAVRIVER hospitals taken on the strength - Lieut Col P. MOXEY, having completed S. appointed A.D.M.S.	Ph
"	7.12.16		1 N.C.O. and 29 men from the 2/wos.R. Field Ambulance attached for duty. Eight men returned from Wagon Lines whilst the Ambulance. Three men wounded & C.C.S.	Ph Ph
"	8.12.16		Capt. ROBSON returned from the A.D.S. at DANUBE TRENCH to the Divisional Rest Station at VARENNES. Lieut Nase rank also relieved. Attended a Conference at IVth CORPS Headquarters	Ph

WAR DIARY
or
INTELLIGENCE SUMMARY.
(Erase heading not required.)

Army Form C. 2118.

Place	Date	Hour	Summary of Events and Information	Remarks and references to Appendices
VARENNES	9.12.16		A further supply of 12 men sent out to obtain supply of S.A.A. fuel at the Divisional Reft Station being only sufficient for eight hours; and it being necessary to obtain further supply for heating huts in Lieutenant obtained further supplies.	O.K.
	10.12.16		The Reft Station was visited by the D.M.S. 5th ARMY who expressed his satisfaction with the progress being made.	O.K.
"	11.12.16		Sixteen men at the A.D.S. (DANUBE TRENCH) relieved by a similar party from CABSTAND. Reft Station at VARENNES visited by the D.M.S. IVth CORPS. who wished me to send all but the minimum cases of illness to Casualty Clearing Station as the accommodation there was not available for convalescence.	O.K.
"	12.12.16		Routine work.	O.K.
"	13.12.16		Inspection of huts, equipment &c.	O.K.
"	14.12.16		Lieut. MARRIOTT returned from duty with 2/7 Warwicks.	O.K.

Army Form C. 2118.

WAR DIARY
or
INTELLIGENCE SUMMARY.
(Erase heading not required.)

Instructions regarding War Diaries and Intelligence Summaries are contained in F. S. Regs., Part II. and the Staff Manual respectively. Title pages will be prepared in manuscript.

Place	Date	Hour	Summary of Events and Information	Remarks and references to Appendices
VARENNES	15.12.16		Lieut MARRIOTT detached for duty with the 2/1st Gloucesters. Lieut NASE replaces Capt CORNELIUS at the A.D.S.	Ph
"	16.12.16		Divine service at A.D.S. relieved by a similar party from CABSTAND.	Ph
"	17.12.16		Capt HALLETT arrived as reinforcement.	Ph
"	18.12.16		Routine work. Visit from D.D.M.S. 14th Corps. Capt WOOD proceeded to A.D.S. Capt CORNELIUS taking charge at CABSTAND.	Ph
"	19.12.16		Lecture on Gas Respirators by Sergt Sevier.	Ph
"	20.12.16		Visit by D.M.S. 4th Army. Routine work.	Ph
"	21.12.16		Routine work.	Ph
"	22.12.16		Capt HALLETT replaces Capt CORNELIUS at CABSTAND, Capt CORNELIUS proceeding to 2/8th Worcesters for duty.	Ph
"	23.12.16		Lieut NASE attached to 307th Brigade R.F.A. for duty.	Ph
"	24.12.16		Lieut STUART attached to the Ambulance for duty.	Ph
"	25.12.16		Lieut LENNAN sent to 2/5th Gloucesters as M.O. 20 of the personnel A.D.S. relieved by a similar number from VARENNES.	Ph
"	26.12.16		Lieut HART is returned through.	Ph

Army Form C. 2118.

WAR DIARY
of
INTELLIGENCE SUMMARY.
(Erase heading not required.)

Instructions regarding War Diaries and Intelligence Summaries are contained in F. S. Regs., Part II. and the Staff Manual respectively. Title pages will be prepared in manuscript.

Place	Date	Hour	Summary of Events and Information	Remarks and references to Appendices
VARENNES	27-12-16		Evacuation of A.D.S. about by a similar number from CABSTAND Rendezvous.	Ply
"	28-12-16		Lieut MARRIOTT signs mess and proceeds to England on termination of his contract.	Ply / Ply
"	29-12-16		Medical Board held at VARENNES. Quarters A.D.M.S. Lieut MARRIOTT (6A) Capt MARRIOTT Eng of gas in field hospital return to permanent	Ply / Ply
"	30-12-16		Headquarters ceases to be a Divisional Rest Station 107 Cases transferred from VARENNES to the newly formed CORPS REST STATION at EAST CHAIRPAYE. Lieuts STUART & HART and	Ply / Ply
"	31-12-16		21 other ranks detailed for duty at the latter place.	

P. Morey Lieut Col Harvey

O.C. 2/2 S.M. Field Ambulance

Ephemeral

140/9 + Vol 9

War Diary

S.M.O.
2/3 Field Ambulance. 61st Division

January 1917.

Volume 9.

COMMITTEE FOR THE
MEDICAL HISTORY OF THE WAR
Date 13 MAR. 1917

WAR DIARY
or
INTELLIGENCE SUMMARY

Army Form C. 2118.

Place	Date	Hour	Summary of Events and Information	Remarks and references to Appendices
VARENNES	1.1.17		Routine duties. Capt. HALLETT proceeded to DANUBE TRENCH R31.C6.8. Capt WOOD	WVW
	2.1.17		to CABSTAND W10.C.5.3.	WVW
	3.1.17		Routine duties. Improving sanitation.	WVW
	4.1.17		Routine duties	WVW
	5.1.17		Routine duties	WVW
	6.1.17		Capt SCANLAN proceeded to CAPOSTANO. Capt. WOOD to VARENNES. Pres. d.2.4.	WVW
			DDMS + ADMS visited the ambulance. Capt. ROBSON proceeded on leave. Gave up	WVW
			DONNET'S POST X.7.A.0.2.	WVW
	7.1.17		Visit by ADMS & Sanitary officers.	WVW
	8.1.17		Routine duties.	WVW
	9.1.17		Lt. NASE attached to 2/5 GLOSTERS.	WVW
	10.1.17		Routine duties.	WVW
			DMS inspected ambulance. Four reinforcements arrived.	WVW
	11.1.17		ADMS visit.	WVW
	12.1.17		ADMS visit. Capt WOOD attached temporarily 1/1. BUCKS.	WVW
	13.1.17		Routine duties. 2 stretcher parties 5.6 F. Amb. arrived.	WVW
	14.1.17			WVW

Army Form C. 2118.

WAR DIARY
or
INTELLIGENCE SUMMARY.
(Erase heading not required.)

Instructions regarding War Diaries and Intelligence
Summaries are contained in F.S. Regs., Part II.
and the Staff Manual respectively. Title pages
will be prepared in manuscript.

Place	Date	Hour	Summary of Events and Information	Remarks and references to Appendices
VARENNES.	15.6.17		Headquarters taken over by 56.F.Amb.	WVW
BEAUQUESNES.	16.6.17		O.C. evacuated to CCS. Ambulance (Col. VARENNES) to BEAUQUESNES.	WVW
			CAPT. SCANLAN relieved CAPT. WOOD with 2/1 Bucks. CAPT. WOOD taken temporary command of the Ambulance.	WVW
LE MEILLARD	17.6.17		Ambulance proceeded to LE MEILLARD. During the previous week (and the SEASP) motor ambulances had been also sent there to [?] first to [?] initiated the transport with us the [?]	WVW
CONTEVILLE.	18.6.17		Ambulance proceeded from LE MEILLARD to CONTEVILLE.	WVW
L'ABBAYE D'AUMONT FARM.	19.6.17		CONTEVILLE to L'ABBAYE D'AUMONT FARM.	WVW
	20.6.17		Started work as detailed for advance of the Divisional Rest Station des Scories Hospital. Visit by ADMS.	WVW
	21.6.17		Routine duties. Construction. Installation.	WVW
	22.6.17		"	WVW
	23.6.17		"	WVW
			Box latrines & refuse buckets emptied & disinfected daily. All equipment cleaned, checked & deficiencies noted. Transport overhauled. Inspection of feet.	WVW

WAR DIARY
INTELLIGENCE SUMMARY

Army Form C. 2118.

Place	Date	Hour	Summary of Events and Information	Remarks and references to Appendices
L'AB BAYE			Funeral took place during afternoon.	WVW
D'AMMONT	24.1.17.		Visit from ADMS 9. Conference. Routine duties.	WVW
FARM.	25.1.17.		DDMS visited ambulance. Conference. Routine duties.	WVW
	26.1.17		Routine duties. Capt. HALLETT detailed for a course of instruction with 11th Sanitary Section.	WVW
	27.1.17.		Lt. HART proceeds on leave.	WVW
	28.1.17.		Construction of work in kitchen, washhouse, rifle rack in transport villa, walk from Wn. house of ablution & latrine for battn.	WVW
	29.1.17.		Routine duties. Divisional sports.	WVW
	30.1.17.		—	WVW
	31.1.17.		—	WVW

W W(?)
Capt RAMC

140/94

Confidential

Vol 10

61/124

War Diary

of

2/3 Field Ambulance 61st Div.

O. of February 28th 1917.

From February 1st 1917.

(Volume 10)

COMMITTEE FOR THE
MEDICAL HISTORY OF THE WAR
Date 4 — APR.1917

WAR DIARY
INTELLIGENCE SUMMARY

Army Form C. 2118.

2/3 South Midland Field Ambulance
GrDiv

Place	Date	Hour	Summary of Events and Information	Remarks and references to Appendices
L'ABBAYE	Feb. 1st		Routine duties.	
D'ARMONT FARM	2		" " Warning order / move received.	
	3		OC 2/4th Field Ambulance called in reference to taking over the wagons of C(??) giving instructions to Blanket Supply party by Bujore, ordered this evening to remove overnight. Instructed totals 16 cars 1 section 1 to 3 sections with wagons. Instructed totals 16 cars 1 section 1 to 3 sections with sections.	
	4		A.D.M.S. inspected Section & Then sick.	
L'ETOILE	4		Marched off with ambulances from L'ABBAYE D'ARMONT at 11–30 a.m. arrived to within a mile on some billetings & instructions made by the owner, sent on (also sent to L'ETOILE. Took on some empty houses (in a hospital men billeted also in empty houses. Instructed to evacuate any sick or wounded sick to AUBEVILLE. Four DAMVILLERS cars arrived at L'ETOILE in the evening to replace (our DEASY cars left at the workshop. Hey(??) general.	
	5		Routine duties.	
	6		" " Lt SMART detailed to attend 476 Coy RE billets in the village.	
	7		" " Capt METCALFE & LT YOUNG reported for duty. A car has been sent with them from CLAIRFAYE under instructions from ADMS.	

WAR DIARY
INTELLIGENCE SUMMARY.
(Erase heading not required.)

Army Form C. 2118.

Place	Date	Hour	Summary of Events and Information	Remarks and references to Appendices
L'ÉTOILE	Feb 8.		Routine duties. Inspection of recruits.	
	– 9.		– LT LENNAN reported for duty from LA TOUQUET where he has been in hospital.	
			CAPT HALLETT detailed for duty with DCHI. (Temporary leave duties).	
	–10		Routine duties. CAPT ROBSON detailed (a temporary duty with 2/c BERKS. under instructions from A.D.M.S. hospital was inspected & received a visitation at 6 p.m. All cases with the exception of 3 cases were ordered to ABBEVILLE C.C.S. Car was on detail for duty with 307 Bde. R.A.	
	–11.		No [further] one after 12 a.m. LT BROOKES as Transport Officer & LT LENNAN started at 10.20 a.m. with all the horse transport two days in advance of remainder of unit & move proceeding by route to MARCELCAVE. They carried three days rations.	
	–12		No horse after 12 a.m. Horses [or] other in [or inspection] in full [marching] order.	
	–13		Entrained at LONGPRE. Lorry took over the blankets & (no sheets to strike). Detrained	
MARCELCAVE			at MARCELCAVE and marched to 101 Camp. Billeted in wooden huts.	
	–14.		CAPT SCANLON returned from temporary duty with BUCKS. 2/1st. General fatigues.	
	–15.		Transport marched on to camp. General fatigues.	
	–16		Short march with whole unit to HARBONNIÈRES. Took over a large building in	

WAR DIARY
INTELLIGENCE SUMMARY.

Place	Date	Hour	Summary of Events and Information	Remarks and references to Appendices
HARBONNIERES	Feb. 16.		The town which consists principally of cottages which are very badly lit and (not studied as) accomodate. A considerable number of men billeted without bedding or blankets in cottages of 100 or so. Cases in which number of men billeted in cottages suffering in some cases from in fact, or simply (sick) whose evacuation of necessary to HARCOURT. Some details sent to cottages (cattle sheds) to construct bedsteads.	
	17.			
	18.		French Soldiers (sick) whose evacuation necessary to HARCOURT. Some details sent to cottages (cattle sheds) to construct bedsteads. Routine work, lectures, practice.	
	19.		Routine duties.	
	20.		—	
	21.		—	
	22.		LT HART detailed for duty with 61. DIV. TRAIN. Works construction of new incinerator.	
	23.		Added to cookhouse system. Thatched type of large hut. 1 mile away from hospital in VAUVILLERS road. As patients arrive at these us later there, the Neo + fair unit can be brought to bear.	
	24		Routine duties. LT. YOUNG reconnaissance from AMIS details gives out, of COYS 35°. Bio.	
	25.		CAPT SCOTT arrived to take command.	

WAR DIARY
or
INTELLIGENCE SUMMARY.

(Erase heading not required.)

Army Form C. 2118.

Place	Date	Hour	Summary of Events and Information	Remarks and references to Appendices
HARBONNIERS	26.2.17.		Took over command of Hill Ambulance from Capt. WOOD RAMC (T.F). Capt. LANDER. RAMC (T.F) arrived for temporary duty and taken on the strength.	
"	27.2.17		Attended Comdg. Officers meeting recieved instructions for A. & B. Wainstein A.D.M.S. IV Corps orders Div Main Dressing Station. Issued order detailing Officer for in charge of medicines occupied wards & detailing for materials.	
"	28.2.17		Capt. SCANLAN. RAMC (T.F) detailed for temporary duty with 307 Bde R.F.A. Issued order for Capt. LANDER to relieve tomorrow & assume medical charge of 2/5 Glosters Regt.	

J.W.Scott Capt. R.A.M.C.
O.C. 2/3 S.M. H. Amb.

140/2042

CONFIDENTIAL Vol XI

61st Div

COMMITTEE FOR THE
MEDICAL HISTORY OF THE WAR
Date 11 MAY 1917

WAR DIARY
OF THE 2/3RD FIELD AMBULANCE

VOLUME

MARCH 1 TO 31. 1917.

WAR DIARY — 2/3 SOUTH MIDLAND FIELD AMBULANCE

Army Form C. 2118

Reference map: ROSIERES

INTELLIGENCE SUMMARY

Place	Date	Hour	Summary of Events and Information	Remarks and references to Appendices
HARBONNIERES	1/3/17		Sent two motor ambulances to OC 7/8 & A.D. VAUVILLERS. Stretcher bearer dispatch completed. 422 blankets	
"	2/3/17		D.D.M.S. IV Corps visited Divisional training station. (2/2 S.M. & Aff. OC 7/3 S.M. & Ant.)	
"	3/3/17		Capt. SCANLON R.A.M.C. (T.C.) returned from duty with 307 Bde. R.F.A.	
"	4/3/17		Took over Adrian Huts in VAUVILLERS, now extra accommodation for 52 patients.	
"			Capt. HART R.A.M.C. (T.C.) reports to detention hospital with 36 Div. Revise IV Corps hoisting arrangements.	
"			2.0 Lt HANNEY 2/3 Ack Ill through a skylight, fractures skull, wounded to CCS. B.117 received.	
"	5/3/17		Interted in A.D. new store for casualty stretchers & loads for detention hospital.	
"	6/3/17		A.D.M.S. IV Corps inspected hospital. Submitted returns under G.R.O. 1198 for equipment to recent but.	
"	7/3/17		Second checking orders in case for Yeo. Going chimneys in continual.	
"	8/3/17		Capt. HALLET & Capt. ROBSON, chief of the strength of the unit. Ordered to draw two Sayers stones & materials for making seats and handles.	

WAR DIARY
INTELLIGENCE SUMMARY.

Army Form C. 2118.

(Erase heading not required.)

Instructions regarding War Diaries and Intelligence Summaries are contained in F.S. Regs., Part II. and the Staff Manual respectively. Title pages will be prepared in manuscript.

Place	Date	Hour	Summary of Events and Information	Remarks and references to Appendices
HARBONNIERES.	8/3/17 (cont.)		to Kents for functions (later) asked to attend. to draw it for our extn. for hospital	Appx 6
"	9/3/17.		Received 100 blankets & 40 mattresses from 36.C.C.S. Stores dumped, dumpy: 119 blankets. Above 11 were empty, taking 50 blankets.	Appx 7. Appx 8.
"	10/3/17		Paid repatriation. Mar- sick offices down to rest. to 2/1 F.A. GUILLACOURT.	Appx 9.
"	11/3/17		Two boat accidents. (a) on stretcher & 2.O.R, 3 Cpy. 61 Div. trans (1) several men from 2/5 Warwick, all removed to 13.C.C.S.	
"	12/3/17		Returned 100 blankets to 36.C.C.S. Hospital linen and harness with 2 h" D.D.M.S. IV Corps visited hospital and huts.	
"	13/3/17		Capt. W. V. WOOD A.A.M.C. (T.F.) 2/5 F.A. sick in quarters, influenza. Took over home with few rooms (accommodation?) a reasonable number.	Appx 10.
"	14/3/17		" " Military HOSPICE carefully accommodating 20 cases. 6. Wood at char-of divisional cases, 9 dysenteric arrangements made. Kit and clothing inspection of the whole unit.	Appx 11.

WAR DIARY

INTELLIGENCE SUMMARY

(Erase heading not required.)

Army Form C. 2118.

Place	Date	Hour	Summary of Events and Information	Remarks and references to Appendices
HARBONNIERES	14/3/17 (contd)		Body of a dead man admitted 1 P.M, a transport to 2/2 F.A. for P.M. & burial.	
"	15/3/17		Charges for the 1000 received for A.A. & Q. mg in reference 9 loan. D.D.G. BROOKES proceeded with dept. officers to lease location of hospital and huts.	M.W.F
"	16/3/17		Col PICKARD A.D.M.S. 61 Div visited. A.D.M.S's instructions to evacuate minor cases to C.C.S. Arranged to give all surplus equipment at HOSPICE in lieu of a proper store. Cpl WIDMAN to be in charge.	M.W.F
"	17/3/17		Division conference J.O.C.s F.Amb. & A.D.M.S's Office. Arranged a definite scheme for dealing with a large number of casualties at HARBONNIERES. R.A.M.C. order no 13 of A.D.M.S. received. Arranged to send A.D.S. at LIHONS however with O.C. 2/2 F.A.	M.W.F
"	18/3/17		Received order to offer - surplus store at HOSPICE. Operation orders no 14 received. 2/3 F.A. to remain at HARBONNIERES as also Div Main Dressing Station	M.W.F

WAR DIARY or INTELLIGENCE SUMMARY.

(Erase heading not required.)

Army Form C. 2118.

Place	Date	Hour	Summary of Events and Information	Remarks and references to Appendices
HARBONNIERES	18/3/17 (contd)		Orders received to administer Anti Tetanic serum to M.D.S. and at A.D.S. Substitution in gas helmets now completed. All latrines emptied. Adrian Huts fitted as cubicles to be equipped as HOSPICE. Operation Order No. 15 issued	appx
"	19/3/17		Lt. STUART detailed for temporary duty at IV Corps H.Qrs. Operation order No. 16 issued	appx
"	20/3/17		No further cases to be sent to Divl. Rest Station 2/1 F.A. at GUILLACOURT. No Scabies cases to be admitted to HAMC.	
"	21/3/17		Capt. A.G.T. FISHER R.A.M.C (T.F.) reports his arrival of posting to "B" Section. Closed down second hut – cubicles all patients in first hut. Orders received to evacuate to 36 C.C.S. CAYEUX	appx
"	22/3/17		A.D.M.S. 61 Div. brought in semi conscious at 1.30 a.m. received peacefully evacuated to 36 C.C.S. Lt. D.O.R. reports to O.C. 2/1 at GUILLACOURT to take over new subsidiary room at WIENCOURT. Capt. FISHER detailed to attend sick daily.	appx
"	23/3/17		3 persons bathing – 3 clothes bathing – 2 shower water cases sent to A.D.M.S	appx

WAR DIARY
INTELLIGENCE SUMMARY

Army Form C. 2118.

Place	Date	Hour	Summary of Events and Information	Remarks and references to Appendices
HARBONNIERES	24/3/17		Had all hill tents & operating tents pitched. There will tents unserviceable. D.D.M.S. visited hospital. Sick convoy received on tour at 11 P.M.	
"	25/3/17		Attended medical board on Major TAYLOR after "Derby". Stoker disinfector disinfecting blankets & mud. Sent 9 A.D. book to D.A.G. 2nd Echelon. A.D.M.S notifies unit.	over
"	26/3/17		Previous morning orders to proceed to FALVY tomorrow.	
"	27/3/17		Operation order No 16 received. Reconnoitred roads to FALVY. 3rd & 9th BROOKES returned from leave.	over
"	28/3/17		Closed hospital at HARBONNIERES 6.36 a.m. & to duty. Moved Hq Amb by road to FALVY.	
"	29/3/17		D/- LENNAN & 10R lef? Unit to attend nicks in the district of HARBONNIERES. When employed to establishment left & Capt WIDMAN to hand in Schwiesp. Unit. Sent Daimler can to HAR BONNIERES for one D/- LENNAN	over
FALVY	30/3/17		Sent 2 Daimler & 2 subsidise to O.C. 2/2 F.A. ATHIES	over

WAR DIARY
INTELLIGENCE SUMMARY

Army Form C. 2118.

Place	Date	Hour	Summary of Events and Information	Remarks and references to Appendices
FALVY	31/3/17		Sun'd ainte can returned by O.C. 2/1 FA Q.G. SMITH A.S.C. a motor cycle attached for time unit to A.D.M.S. Sgt-10 pain fumes have been ordered to BETHEN COURT to arrest & supplying put Moved to 32 A.D. med Stores for materials for preventilating in wells	J.W.W. MPG & other O.C. 2/3 S.M. F. Amb.

CONFIDENTIAL

61st Div.

WAR DIARY

OF

2/3RD SOUTH MIDLAND FIELD AMBULANCE

FROM APRIL 1st 1917 TO APRIL 30TH 1917

VOLUME

COMMITTEE FOR THE
MEDICAL HISTORY OF THE WAR
Date − 6 JUN. 1917

Army Form C. 2118.

WAR DIARY

INTELLIGENCE SUMMARY.

(Erase heading not required.)

2/3 S.M. Fd Amb.
61st Div

Reference Map
62 TS. }
62 C.   } 1/40,000
66 D. }

Place	Date	Hour	Summary of Events and Information	Remarks and references to Appendices
FALVY	1.4.17.		Sgt. I. McC. O. 10 men from fwd station to 2/1 FA BETHENCOURT to assist in pitching marquees. Operation order no. 10 received from A.D.M.S. Ordered Capt. METCALFE, Capt. FISHER, one tent subdivision, one horse ambulance, two Daimler cars, one operating tent, 2 hosp tents with necessary medical equipment to form a part of TREFCON. 2 Capt. SCANLON, Capt. WOOD (2/1FA), one horse ambulance to form an A.D.S. at VILLEVEQUE. Tent subdivision and horse ambulance to bivouac at W.6.C.7/1FA to be ready.	All June I [initials]
"	2.4.17	5.39am	Capt. METCALFE reported main dressing war established at W.9.b.9.4.	
		"	A.D.S. d. TREFCON and A.D.S. at VILLEVEQUE	
		"	W.12.d.8.9.	
			Shrapnel front d. TREFCON and A.D.S. d. VILLEVEQUE. Sent 7 Ford car to A.D.S. d. VILLEVEQUE to run between Main-place and infantrymen trench at W.11.C.3.8. Sent a Daimler car with 4 bearers to carry our cases at W.11.C.3.8. and bring back wounded to fwd d. TREFCON.	

Army Form C. 2118.

WAR DIARY
or
INTELLIGENCE SUMMARY.
(Erase heading not required.)

Instructions regarding War Diaries and Intelligence Summaries are contained in F. S. Regs., Part II. and the Staff Manual respectively. Title pages will be prepared in manuscript.

Place	Date	Hour	Summary of Events and Information	Remarks and references to Appendices
FALVY.	2/4/17 (contd)		Sent the remainder of "B" Section men and transport to A.D.S. at TREFCON at 2 P.M. Received orders from ADMS at 7.15 P.M. to U.Col. SCANLON who is to establish advanced post in the cellar at R27C84 with 20 men to maintain link with 2/1 M.O. Sect. 10 men from TREFCON to relieve 16 Cy. W00D at VILLEVEQUE.	W/S
TREFCON	3/4/17		Visited hd. of TREFCON, and A.D.S. at VILLEVEQUE and R.27c. Received orders from A.D.M.S. 1.30 P.M. to move the remainder of FALVY to TREFCON and to ... Planet 7 P.M. Arranged for a lorry to take the advanced post X.21 R.78. left here with the two cars that were carrying on the work. Fine day. Lt. Col. Withers at FALVY with complete equipment covered load all day. Visited A.D.S at VILLEVEQUE and at R.27C. Sent a second Horse car to R27C.	W/S
"	4/4/17		Opened up at TREFCON as a main dressing station. Am bulance waggons to work between in ville B A.D. Stty. Evacuation on any car cars to 2/1 F.A. at BETHENCOURT.	

WAR DIARY or INTELLIGENCE SUMMARY

Army Form C. 2118.

Place	Date	Hour	Summary of Events and Information	Remarks and references to Appendices
TREFCON	2/4/17 (cont)		13 hours a.g. wounded civilians evacuated to report to Mr O.S.S. night of left Roisel also BOIS HOLNON and MAISSEMY evacuated. Orders received at 7 p.m. to open an A.D.S. at Rouge-in Cottage BOIS d'HOLNON by 10 p.m. Capt. SCANLON detailed to do this. Orders Capt. WORDE from A.D.S. in Outils moved up Capt SCANLON at R 27 c. Evacuation from ROUGE COLLEGE through-wood to MARTEVILLE in R 35 a. D Sect— a – R 33 r – c. by Ford ambulance. Sect 10 extra men & A.D.S. of Outils R 27 c. Sect bus used ambulance to help 6 Capt SCANLON at BOIS d'HOLNON.	
"	3/4/17		Moved to R 27 c. One Daimler Car (B) move to the outside of TREFCON and sent to join the unit at MARTEVILLE. Put room 1 oth A.D.S. is called at H.Q. 103 Bde in station. 10th the 18th A.D.S. will be little wounded received from D.I.E.A. Capt FISHER of party relieved Capt SCANLON's party at Rouge-in Cottage. 11.30 p.m. Ordered 10th A.D.S. orders Capt SCANLON to move his party to Rouge-in Cottage	
"	4/4/17			

WAR DIARY
or
INTELLIGENCE SUMMARY.

Army Form C. 2118.

Place	Date	Hour	Summary of Events and Information	Remarks and references to Appendices
TREFCON	6/4/17 (am)		(with) West-ward reconn.[?] of the hill. 3 Ford Cars & 2 Daimlers [?] on employ from d. MARTEVILLE; 3 handed over to d. VILLECHOLLE & 2 at Bois d'HOLNON. ADMS visited TREFCON. Col. FISHER reported AD.S. at Bois d'HOLNON Still [?] to now wounded & stretcher bills[?]. Maj. ADSS quartermaster Newspaper.	
"	7/4/17		10.2 Pm relieving 163 Div. Cav.[?] Sec. 4 began to clear d. MARTEVILLE at off load cars, road bad & [?] orders. Snapshot left ADSS. Capt. LINNAH & Daimler car returned to TREFCON from detached duty at HARBONNIERES. Col. METCALFE party arrived 1.30 pm to relieve Col. WOOD & party d. GRICOURT[?] ADMS visits ambulance. One Daimler cars & Wolsen out of its orders d. VILLEVEQUE run to a team[?] gun belonging the way & caught it. Had carried on to advance d. Fountaine Col. & there (Col) FISHER to send 2 motor lorries and lories from W. HOLMON 6[?]	yes

WAR DIARY
or
INTELLIGENCE SUMMARY.

(Erase heading not required.)

Army Form C. 2118.

Place	Date	Hour	Summary of Events and Information	Remarks and references to Appendices
TREFCON	7/4/17 (ct)	0417	Road crossing at MARTEVILLE. Visits 1st R.H. Division advance area of all of stations down under ADS. Sector with Smith and Gen. Carlo Car stacked you to MARTEVILLE, other Capt. FISHER in with advance line at L. ADS and CRITICAL Capt. FISHER had to move the ADS to called R.34a. as the quarry was beginning to be a gun position. Capt. and 2 am and new who did shell the between LSRHL & ADSat R.34.c.	W.G. MNS
"	7/4/17		Capt. METCALFE should at 11 km ADS at shrine of VILLOCHOLLE and moved to new hut at R.27L. Address the 4 men stations & orders at MARTEVILLE. Attend ADMS president the ADSs. ADMS 35 Div called at H.qrs at TREFCON and am capable of evacuation with him. X.m. A.C. Cloud M.S.sh 3.45 pm. Sent to heaven to hand carry am explicit of VILLEVEQUE owing to staff issue	W.G.s

WAR DIARY or INTELLIGENCE SUMMARY.

Army Form C. 2118.

Place	Date	Hour	Summary of Events and Information	Remarks and references to Appendices
TREFCON	19/4/17		OC POWELL OC 106 FA 35 Div came to TREFCON to make arrangements for taking over MDS & tw ADSs. Sgt. on reconn. back with OC 106 FA to OFFY & taken in marquees. Forwarded application for and awarded a Red Rosette. " recommendation for Capt. FISHER for Military Cross Hail, snow & sleet again. Received orders from ADMS to proceed to DOUILLY after handing over MDS & ADS to 106 FA Sent orders to Capt. Mitchell & Capt. FISHER to hand over ADSs & proceed to DOUILLY. 12½ pm – 5 O.R. 106 FA advanced party arrived 6.30 pm. Sgt. Capt. SCANLON & advance party at 8 am to DOUILLY. MDS hand over ADSs with OC 106 FA. Handed over MDS & TREFCON & two ADSs to 106 FA. Marched at 10 pm to DOUILLY. Personnel from two ADSs arrived at DOUILLY 8 pm. Snowing hard.	AH WPJ
DOUILLY	19/4/17			

WAR DIARY
or
INTELLIGENCE SUMMARY.
(Erase heading not required.)

Army Form C. 2118.

Place	Date	Hour	Summary of Events and Information	Remarks and references to Appendices
DOUILLY	11/4/17	(am)	Arranged to billet each of 182 Fd Amb in hand at barn. Lt STUART church ff Bd strength of the unit took on billets recce'd & 7 wounds a buttled for each capable of accommodating 160 men. D.D.M.S. I/C of overall unit	A/F
	12/4/17		Rain & Snow	
	13/4/17		Received 1500 from held ambu. at NESLE Capt. E. H. WOOD detailed for duty with ADS Worcesters vice Cpt MANUEL sick off.	gult
	14/4/17		Received orders from A.D.M.S. to move 10ft will bill. out-div (members) to report NOCX MAC LANGUEVOISIN, the other buildings to take over. Capt MCTCALFE of (cont) W/4 of 1 Pr A. Visit ADMS + SDMS. Arranged with SDMS to leave party at LANGUEVOISIN, taking in 107 Fd ot NESLE. The party to work under orders of 107 FA as an annexe. Capt FISHER ordered to refurbish will we leave-ours-div. w/cars (a room arranged) 2:30 P.M. to O/C 32nd Div MDS at FORESTE.	A/F

Army Form C. 2118.

WAR DIARY
~~INTELLIGENCE SUMMARY.~~
(Erase heading not required.)

Instructions regarding War Diaries and Intelligence Summaries are contained in F. S. Regs., Part II. and the Staff Manual respectively. Title pages will be prepared in manuscript.

Place	Date	Hour	Summary of Events and Information	Remarks and references to Appendices
DOULLY	14/4/17 (ctd)		Visited 32" Div M.D.S. at FORESTE and ect ADMS 32 Div. ADMS 61 Div (Col HOWKINS) called with General. Paid the unit. Checked equipment of A.D. Section. 6 lot equipment sent to LANGUEVOISIN. Sent 3 Daimlers & 1 Ford at 10 P.M. with 2 days rations & drivers & orderlies to report to DDMS VII Corps. FA at NESLE.	
"	15/4/17		Capt. FISHER and horse amb-div held "422" Div returned	
"	16/4/17		ADMS ranks ambulance and inspects the men on parade. Sent 6 wheeled stretchers on loan to 105 FA. 35 Div. 3 Daimlers & 1 Ford returned by 107 FA 36 Div	
"	17/4/17		Sgt GREEN sent to 107 FA for conducting return of men of 61st Div admitted to 107 FA	
"	18/4/17		ModC 92 FA and SADMS 6 Div and meal - routes medical arrangements (hand-over) of 32 Div	
"	19/4/17		Lieut LENNAN and Horse amb-div left DOULLY on road to SAVY to take over ADS from 32 Div. Operation order No 25 received from ADMS. 61st Div relieving 32 Div on 19, 20 & 21 April.	

WAR DIARY or INTELLIGENCE SUMMARY

Place	Date	Hour	Summary of Events and Information	Remarks and references to Appendices
DOUILLY	19/4/17 (contd)		Sgt. T.M.C.O. & 12.O.R to report to O.C. 92 F.A. at FORESTE to look after stores. Capt. METCALFE returned from LANGUEVOISIN. Its reminder of 3 wheeled station returned from 105 & 106 F.A. and	
DOUILLY FORESTE	20/4/17		Sub:- Park to Lieut. (Hon. Capt.) SCANLAN & 19 O.R. reported to A.D.S.J. SAVY. Danick arrived for duty from 1, 2, 3 A and. A.D.S.J SAVY heavily shelled last night - chose a new site for then forward South of the gullies present one.	
FORESTE	21/4/17		Sent 3 Danielas & Lords to SAVY by 10 a.m. took over from 1/9 2 F.A. the whole arrangement for clearing and evacuating the line trenches at FORESTE. 13 Marguers, 379 blankets, 152 stretchers. Have now handed over line arrangements to 2/1 F.A.D. DOUILLY. Medical arrangements as follows: M.D.S. at FORESTE. A.D.S. (2 Daniels , 1 ford) SAVY. Relay posts - (16 men 2 wheeled stretchers) HOLNON (west) SAVY X. 29.c.0.5.0. HOLNON S.8.a.5.5 FAYET N.36.c.7.3 " " 8 " " (" ") ( ) S.16.b.4.6. " " 6 " " (A " " have tramway to HOLNON)	

Army Form C. 2118.

WAR DIARY
or
INTELLIGENCE SUMMARY.
(Erase heading not required.)

Instructions regarding War Diaries and Intelligence Summaries are contained in F. S. Regs., Part II. and the Staff Manual respectively. Title pages will be prepared in manuscript.

Place	Date	Hour	Summary of Events and Information	Remarks and references to Appendices
FORESTE	21/4/17 (cont)		R.A.P.s at S.16.c.22. S.16.c.46. M.35.073. Evacuations by car from SAVY – ETREILLERS – VAUX – GERMAINE to FORESTE. From FORESTE to C.C.S. at NESLE & X.M.A.C. on wire to D.D.M.S. IV Corps.	
	22/4/17		Inspected A.D.S. at SAVY & visited 182 Bde H.Qrs. Messrs Sur-Div called FORESTE to 12-1 p.m. 1 FAM. BETHENCOURT. Capt. SCANLON reported about Pte STONE now missing since 10.30 a.m. yesterday. Visited half of GERMAINE.	
"	23/4/17		Arranged about tent-sq treatment of gas cases. Capt. WOOD in charge. Drew 23 500 from field Cashier. Rode to A.D.S. at SAVY.	
"	24/4/17		Was at A.D.S. at SAVY on duty. Had to HOLNON. Attended conference of A.D.M.S. offices. Capt. FISHER relieves Capt. LENNAN at A.D.S. SAVY.	
	25/4/17		Capt LENNAN left – for 10 days leave in England. Accompanied A.D.M.S. to relay pnt. at HOLNON & A.D.S. SAVY. Returned 3.6.0 P.M. to SAVY by Motor Ambulance duty 5/1 F.A.	
	26/4/17		Capt. SCOTT. WILLIAMSON. Z.A.M.C (T.F) arrived for duty.	
	27/4/17		Handed over to Capt. WILLIAMSON.	

Army Form C. 2118.

WAR DIARY
or
INTELLIGENCE SUMMARY.
(Erase heading not required.)

Map Ref. 62 B } 1:40,000
         62 C }
         62 D }

Place	Date	Hour	Summary of Events and Information	Remarks and references to Appendices
	27.4.17		Took over from Lt Col SCOTT visited A.D.S at SAVY — Relief completed by 12 Bgde. Reinspected Roads and A.D.S for Active operations by 182 Bgde.	9/4/1
	28.4.17		Capt SCANLON with drawn to A.D.S. SAVY. (To mend fresh unit.) Routine duties.	9/4/1
	29.4.17		A.D.M.S. inspected Camps. Sectional arrangements/ Ambulance reintroduced. Capt WOOD unit H.Q. Capt FISHER M.C. Wing over A.D.S unit 'C' Section. Capt Mau brung station.	9/4/1
	30.4.17		Capt SCANLON taken over charge B Sectn. Inventories at headquarters shelled out. Relay partial SCANLON again chargy B Section. Sld 61 Map 62 B. 1:40,000. Reconne. Bois de HOUON for Evacuation route. New site selected at point Holwen. Capt FISHER awarded MILITARY CROSS.	9/4/1

Anthony Williamson
Capt. R.A.M.C.T.
Comdg.

CONFIDENTIAL.

WAR DIARY

OF

2/3 S.M. FIELD AMBULANCE.

FROM 1/5/17 TO 31/5/17

(VOLUME)

COMMITTEE FOR THE
MEDICAL HISTORY OF THE WAR
Date 10 JUL. 1917

MEDICAL

Army Form C. 2118.

WAR DIARY
or
INTELLIGENCE SUMMARY.

(Erase heading not required.)

Instructions regarding War Diaries and Intelligence Summaries are contained in F. S. Regs., Part II. and the Staff Manual respectively. Title pages will be prepared in manuscript.

MAP REFERENCES.
AMIENS SHEET 7
LENS   SHEET 11
FRANCE SHEET 51 B
"   "   51 C

Place	Date 1917	Hour	Summary of Events and Information	Remarks and references to Appendices
Jolotu	May 1 1917		Reorganised the Units into Sections. Remnants Capt WOOD to 'A' section, Capt SCANLON to 'B' section, Capt FISHER to 'C' section. Detail of Section such as to allow of 3 sections equipped & manned for A.D.S. work + one section 'A' for Main Dressing Station work. Details in Appendix I. All cars fitted with Thone splinting.	See Appendix I
	May 2		Detailed Constructional work designed for A.D.S.'s on either Sector. For plans etc. see Appendix II	Appendix II
	" 3		Rearranged Tentage at Main Dressing Station FORESTE to permit of every worker well immune of personnel, to seem through way for Cars. 9ft DIKA bridged. Roads reinforced blinks + tentage against wet weather. Dining Room built, also stone an accomodation for sitting cases if need be.	yes
	" 4		Equipment revised, to meet special Surgical requirements. Packing of Panniers altered to allow for carriage of additional material. Details in Appendix III. The use of A.F.W.3210 as a routine measure. Details in Appendix IV.	App III App IV
			Large part of previous days spent in reconnoitring what finds area. A new scheme of evacuation inaugurated with a view to meeting any eventuality. Details Appendix V	App V
			Supervising above alterations & usual Routine + visits to A.D.S.'s	yes
	" 5		do	yes
	" 6		do	yes
	" 7		do	yes
	" 8		do	yes
	" 9		Completed Camouflage of Tentage with Raffia netting. Disinfected of Tested Lorry of w Blankets. Usual Routine + visits Visits A.D.S. Constructional work wire forward.	yes
	" 10		Orders received to evacuate by 13th all Tents, Blankets + other material & eden Corpse large. Visited A.D.S.'s at GP. Sectors with Clef- & Officers of 129 Regiment FRENCH. Explained scheme a methods in use. Gave all information re routes of Evacuation + reason for them use.	yes
	" 11			
	" 12		Men worked excellently well. Ten H.P. small marquees struck + 400 Blankets rolled & despatched to No 21 C.C.S as per Corps orders.	yes

Army Form C. 2118.

WAR DIARY
or
INTELLIGENCE SUMMARY.
(Erase heading not required.)

Instructions regarding War Diaries and Intelligence Summaries are contained in F.S. Regs., Part II. and the Staff Manual respectively. Title pages will be prepared in manuscript.

Place	Date 1917	Hour	Summary of Events and Information	Remarks and references to Appendices
	MAY 13th		Continued despatch of equipment to 2/I.C.F.S. Capt. Ed. WOOD (from 2/1st. E.Anglian) taken in Radius Strength. FRENCH Ambulance & Brancardier officers visited A.D.S.'s again.	(m)
	14		Brigade until the 183 BRIGADE for subsequent move. Conferred with Brigade re handing over & arrangements for move. Medical Board in P.B. men at Headquarters. Billeting Party despatched to NESLE. Warning orders re move & hand over and to O/c A.D.S.'s	(m)
	15		C. Section withdrawn to Headqts. after handing over to FRENCH Stretcher Bearers. Motor Ambulance Cars left at Disposal of FRENCH, eventually to HAM. FRENCH Ambulance take over Site at FORESTE.	(m)
	16		Six D.A.C. mules attached to made up deficiencies in Horses. B. Section withdrawn after handing over to FRENCH, in left sector.	(m) (m)
	17		Moved to MESNIL St NICAISE. an Ambulance & Transport. Arrangements made to carry "Crocks" & unable to walk. Details of "unfit to march" carried thus' Stn. & Ambulance moves in App. VI	App. VI (m)
	18		Personnel entrained to LONGEAU & marched to VILLERS BOCAGE. Transport Brigaded to Divn.s by road. One Medical Officer detailed to accompany Transport column p. Brigade. Motor Ambulance sent to accompany D.A.C. & Artillery Group from MONCHY LAGACHE.	(m)
	19		Capt GOULDING SR taken in Strength. Rested in VILLERS BOCAGE	
	20		Transport rejoined the Unit. Animals very fit & without casualties.	
	21		March to BEAUVAL with Transport.	(m)
	22		Rested.	
	23		Moved to SUS. St LEGER.	(m)
	24		Moved to DAINVILLE with Transport. Personnel carried from Sud. de BAC & DAINVILLE in MOTOR Transport.	(m)

Army Form C. 2118.

WAR DIARY
or
INTELLIGENCE SUMMARY.
(Erase heading not required.)

Instructions regarding War Diaries and Intelligence Summaries are contained in F.S. Regs., Part II. and the Staff Manual respectively. Title pages will be prepared in manuscript.

Place	Date 1917	Hour	Summary of Events and Information	Remarks and references to Appendices
	MAY 25		Camp Camped under Canvas + Bivouac at point Sheet 51C L35d.4.3 on main DOULLENS – ARRAS road. Camp left in pretty condition by preceding unit. Cleaning up occupied day.	App 1
	26		Equipment inspection + general nature. Conference with D.D.M.S. VI Corps.	2
	27		Usual Routine particularly disinfection of men knapsacks & sea provided front aid.	App 3
	28		Usual Routine	do.	App 4
	29		Conferred with O.C. 50th Field Ambulance as to taking over. Warning Notice for Move received.	App 5
	30		Usual routine.	App 6
	31		Packing + Striking camp prepared to move.	App 7

Geo Swan Dennanson Lt Col
O/C 2/3 Sth L'td Amb

APPENDIX I

3rd. Field Ambulance.

The Ambulance is divided into:-

    Headquarters

    "A" Section

    "B" Section

    "C" Section.

Each Section has the full complement of Stretcher Bearers.

"A" Section has additional Nursing Orderlies.

The personnel is divided as follows:-

    Headquarters   18

    "A" Section   62

    "B" & "C" Sections 51 each.

Sgd "Geo Scott Williamson"

Lieut.Col.R.A.M.C.T.
O.C. 2/3rd.S.M.Field Ambulance.

APPENDIX II

Specification to R.E. for Dug-out Dressing Stations at posts:-

The site is in the face of an embankment at each point. Mined galleries are cut into the face of the bank at right angles, so that each gallery allows mining framework to carry 3 stretchers on racks one above the other. The runners are on brackets so that sitting cases can occupy the galleries. The galleries open off a chamber which is roofed with iron shelter sectors, and sandbagged. There are eight galleries at each site.
ACCOMMODATION. 30 lying cases. 50 sitting cases.
or 120 sitting cases.

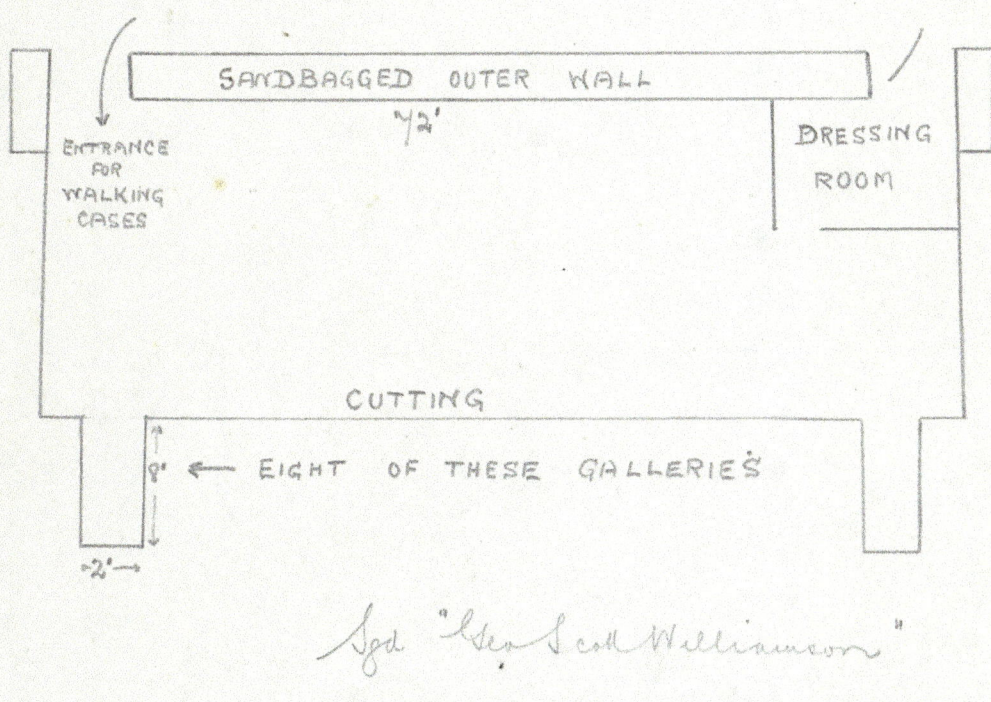

Sgd "Geo Scott Williamson"

Lieut.Col.R.A.M.C.(T)
O.C. 2/3rd S.M. Field Ambulance.

"A" Section.

3rd Field Ambulance.

"A" Pannier.

Primus Stoves	2
Basins.	6
Instrument Trays. 16"x12"	3
Swab bowls.	2 large.
	3 small
Feeders.	3
Funnels.	2
Lane Bags.	2
Boiler.	1
Razors.	4
Scissors.	4
Brushes, Nail.	4
Bowls. $7\frac{1}{4} \times 5\frac{1}{4}$	3
Soap. Carbolic.	6 lbs.
Tow to pack.	
Carrel punch.	1
Rubber tubing.	
Pail for dressings.	1
Plain gauze to pack.	
Thomas Splint extension screws.	20.

===========

APPENDIX III.

Sgd "Geo Scott Williamson"
Lt Col R.A.M.C.
OC 2/3 S. M. F. Amb

"A" Section.

3rd Field Ambulance.

"B" Pannier.

Knives.	20
Forks.	20
Spoons.	20
Pannikins.	30
Plates.	48
Kettle.	1
Pan.	1
Tea pot.	1
Hooks.	6
Basins.washing. 14"	4
Dish cloths.	12
Tow to pack.	
Gauze to pack.	

==========

"A" Section.

3rd Field Ambulance.

"C" Pannier.

Bed pans.	6
Urinals.	6
Washing basins. 11"	18
Brushes,washing.	6
Brushes,white-wash.	4
Hooks,bill.	3
Lines,clothes.	1
Cups,sputum.	6
Barbers kit.	1 Haversack.
Tow to pack.	

==========

Sgd "Geo Scott Williamson"

Lt Col P amb
OC 2/3 S M F Amb

"A" Section.

3rd Field Ambulance.

"D" Pannier.

Towels, hospital.	30
Operating towels.	
Bandages.	
Wool.	
Gauze.	
Ether.	
Chloroform	
Schimmel mask.	1
Gas inhalers.	4
Gas masks.	2
Plaster 2" rolls.	12
1" rolls.	24

= = = = = = = = = =

"A" Section.

3rd Field Ambulance.

"F" Pannier.

Primus stove.	1
Basins. 14"	4
~~Cup, fe~~ Cups, feeding.	5
Funnels.	2
Saucepans.	6
Nail brushes.	2
Basins. 7" x 5"	4
Soap.	2 lbs.
Cups.	10
Hot water bottles.	2
Towels, hospital.	20
Boiler, round.	
Swab bowls.	2

= = = = = = = = = =

Sgd. Geo Scott Williamson
Lt Col R.A.M.C.
O.C. 2/3 S. M. F. Amb.

<u>Theatre Orderly</u>　　　　　<u>3rd. Field Ambulance</u>　　　　<u>B and C Sections.</u>

"A" Pannier.

Primus Stove.	1.
Basins – 14 ins.	2
Instrument Tray.	1
Swab bowl or jar.	1
Feeding Cups.	3.
Funnels.	2.
Sauce pans, EA. Nest.	1
Razor – 1. Scissor – 1	–
Tow – To pack.	2 pkts.
Nail brushes.	2
Basins. 7" x 5¾"	2
Soap, brown windsor.	6 Tabs.
Splints, improvised.	4

==========================

Thomas Splints.	2
Stretcher rails.	2
Splints, various.	–

==========================

Sgd "Geo Scott Williamson"
Lt. Col. R.A.M.C.
O.C. 2/3 Sth. F. Amb.

<u>C O O K S.</u>　　　　　　<u>3rd Field Ambulance.</u>　　　　　<u>B and C. Sections.</u>

<u>"B" Pannier.</u>

Forks, flesh.	2
Knives, table.	10
Forks, table.	10
Spoons, table.	10
Pannikins, pint.	20
Kettle,	1
Ladles.	2
Mincer.	1
Pan.	1
Pot, tea.	1
Hook, bill.	1
Primus Stove.	1
Basins, zinc.	3

= = = = = = = = = = = = = = =

Cocoa - Tea - Milk - Biscuits - Lemco.

To fill.

= = = = = = = = = = = = = = =

"Sgd" Geo. Scott Williamson"
Lieut. Col. Ramsey
O.C. 3/3 S. M. F. Amb.

G.D. Theatre.   3rd Field Ambulance.   B. and C. Sections.

"C" Pannier.

Bed pans.	2
Urinals.	2.
Hot water bottles.	4.
Washing, enamel - 14 in.	2
Brush, scrubbing.	2.
Soap, ordinary.	7 lbs.
Tow.	2 lbs.
White-wash brush.	1
Axe, felling.	1

===============

Tin, Lime. —
Drum, cresol
Bottle, formalin.

===============

Theatre Orderly.   3rd Field Ambulance.   B. and C. Sections.

"D" Pannier.

```
Towels.     Hospital 20 . - Operating. 6

Bandages, roller and triangular )
Wool.                           )  To fill up.
Gauze, plain.                   )

Ether.                             2 lbs.

Chloroform                         2 lbs.

Schimmel Mask.                     1

Plaster, 1 roll 4".
         6 rolls 2"
         6 rolls 1"

Rubber Tourniquets                 3

Eupad (for solution 10 galls)

Tow.                               3 pkts.

Safety pins.                       12 bxs.

Pure Cresol.                       1 Box.

Iodine.                            1 Bottle.

Splints, improvised.               4
```

= = = = = = = = = = = = = = = = =

3rd Field Ambulance.   B. and C. Sections.

"E" Pannier.

Lampman.

Cans oil, Large 1, Small 3.
Lamps, hurricane.   2
Cotton waste.   3 lbs.
Distinguishing flags, pendants, boards.
Lamp, hanging.   1
       = = = = = = = =
Operating Lamp.   "
Flag Poles.   "
Tin of petrol.   "
Tin of Spirit.   "
Drum of oil, burning.   "
Case of Carbide.   "
       = = = = = = = =

Sgd "Geo Scott Williamson"
Lt Col RAMC
OC 3/3 South Mid FA

3rd Field Ambulance.

Carpenters' Chest.

Hammers	2
Chisels.	
Saws etc. etc.	

- - - - - - - - - - -

3rd Field Ambulance.

Reserve Rations.

Case of milk.	
Cases of biscuits.	2
Cases of Bully.	2
Tin of sugar.	
Tin of tea.	

- - - - - - - - - - -

"Sgd" Geo Scott Williamson
Lieut Col Ramc
OC 3/3 S.m.F Amb.

WAR DIARY or INTELLIGENCE SUMMARY

Army Form C. 2118.

MAP REFERENCES: FRANCE Sheet 51c 1/40,000 " LENS 11 1/100,000

Place	Date	Hour	Summary of Events and Information	Remarks and references to Appendices
	JUNE 1st		Moved to from DAINVILLE. (a) Headquarters to ARRAS — HOSPITAL ST JEAN, RUE ST AUBERT. (b) Transport to Racecourse at ⅓ Sheet 51c L.30.a.7.8.	MOVE
	2nd		Unit in Reserve, and refit open out. Cars engaged in collecting sick locally. Capt METCALF detailed for duty with 2/6 GLOSTERS for leave relief. Personnel of a Section engaged in Salvage work under Salvage Officer. 7 O.R. employed at Open Air Bath. 4. 6 O.R. with 2/2 40 AMB.	8pm
ARRAS	3rd		Capt. GOULDING detailed for duty with 306 BDE. R.F.A.	8pm
	4th 5th 6th 7th 8th 9th		Capt FISHER in exchange with Capt GOMPERTZ of 2/6 WARWICKS. Head Qrs moved from ARRAS to Racecourse at Map 51c L.30.a.7.8. in Bivouac. Salvage work & usual Routine of Training.	8pm 8pm 8pm
	10th		Moved to SIMENCOURT SIMENCOURT under 183 INF BRIGADE orders.	MOVE MAP 51c Q.10.d.7.3 8pm
	11th 12th 13th			8pm 8pm
SIMENCOURT	14th 15th 16th		ROUTINE Training in FIRST AID etc.	8pm
	17th		Capt GOMPERTZ detailed for duty with 29 SQUADRON R.F.C.	8pm
	18th 19th 20th		Routine training.	8pm

Army Form C. 2118.

WAR DIARY
or
INTELLIGENCE SUMMARY.
(Erase heading not required.)

Instructions regarding War Diaries and Intelligence Summaries are contained in F. S. Regs., Part II. and the Staff Manual respectively. Title pages will be prepared in manuscript.

Place	Date	Hour	Summary of Events and Information	Remarks and references to Appendices
	JUNE 21		Move from SEMINCOURT to ŒUF (9 Kilometers West ST POL). Transport only. Under 183 INF BRIGADE. Route SEMINCOURT—FREVENT— Bivouac overnight— FREVENT—FILLIÈVRES along main AVESNES—FREVENT—HESDIN ROAD.	
	22		Move of PERSONNEL by TRAIN from GOUY-EN-ARTOIS - TO - HESDIN. By ROAD from HESDIN to ŒUF. Route HESDIN—VIEIL HESDIN—WILLEMAN—ŒUF. Billets in Barns & Cottages. Sick carried to Entraining point & from Detraining pt.	APP I
ŒUF	23		Open ordu to deal with sick of 183 INF BRIGADE in Tentage. Regimental Sick of 183 MGC, TMB & 182 MGC, TMB & Bdg Hq seen daily. Manual Routine Training). Lectures, Company Drill, route marching.	
	24		do	
	25		do	
	26		do	
	27		do Tactical Exercise with ADMS scheme gone over with Officers.	
	28		do	
	29		do	
	30		Competitive sports arranged as part of Physical Training.	

Godwin Williamson
Lt Col. M & SAMC
CUDG 2/3 S.M

APPENDIX 1.

Particulars of those carried during the move on
June 22nd. 1917.

Unit.	Numbers
2/7th. Worcesters	8
2/8th. Worcesters	12
2/4th. Gloucesters	8
2/6th. Gloucesters	8
183rd. Machine Gun Coy.	10
183rd. T.Mortar Battery	1
Total.	47

Appendix IV

A.F.W. 3210, Use of.

(1) The Orderly on each Horse ambulance and Motor ambulance has a supply of these forms and will;
   (a) Fill in particulars of each case intended for the Main Dressing station. Such particulars will include everything asked for on the form, with the exception of the Serial number and the Disease or wound.
   (b) He will mark on the form the class of case such as wounded/lying = w/L, wounded/sitting = w/s, sick/lying = s/L, sick/sitting = s/s.
   (c) He will initial each form in the top left hand corner.
   (d) On arriving at the Main Dressing Station he will hand the A.F.W. 3210 to the Receiving N.C.O.

(2) The receiving N.C.O. will see that he has A.F.W. 3210 for each case, and will direct each case to their respective accommodation, viz, lying or sitting cases, sick or wounded.

(3) The forms will next be handed to the M.O. who will fill in the nature of the disease or wound and also mark the disposal of the case, i.e. ccs/L, ccs/s, crs/L, crs/s, remain/L, remain/s, Dental Specialist=S/D, Eye Specialist = S/E.
   The M.O. will also mark as to A.T.S. or any other drugs administered.

(4) The A & D clerk will then check through the particulars with each case and entry will be made in the A & D book. A.F.W. 3118a (Field Medical card) will then be made out and the A & D serial number added to both Field Medical card and A.F.W. 3210.

(5) When the A.F.W. 3210 are complete they will be put into bundles for C.C.S. and C.R.S. and handed to the evacuation N.C.O.

(6) The evacuation N.C.O. will ensure that he does not evacuate any case for whom he has no A.F.W. 3210. When convoy has been disposed of he will hand into the Receiving Room A.Fs.W. 3210 in bundles, pinned, and will initial each bundle.

(7) Not until the A.Fs.W. 3210, initialled by the Evacuation N.C.O., have been returned to the Receiving room will the A & D clerk mark off the cases in the A & D book.

Sgd "Geo. Scott Williamson"
Lieut Col R.A.M.C.
OC 2/3 S.M.F. Amb.

APPENDIX V

TO. A.D.M.S.,　　　　　　　　　　　　　SECRET.
　　　　61st. Division.

Map Reference 62.B. & 62.C. = 1 - 40,000.

1. I beg to report the following dispositions.

   (i). Alterations necessitated by

   (a). Redistribution and arrangement of Troops holding the line.

   (b). Alteration in the traffic routes as per Divisional & Brigade Orders.

   (c). Front is divided into Right & Left Sectors. Dividing line approximately from ETREILLER (62.C.) to point S.11 central including FRANCILLY.

   Regimental Aid Posts remain the same.

2. Two Advanced Dressing Stations, one for each Sector established.

   Right Section, at SAVY on ETREILLERS - SAVY Road at point (62.C) X.29.d.4.5. (Position not altered)

   Left Section, on the ATTILLY - HOLNON Road at point (62.C) X.11.a.0.2.

   Relay Posts.　Right Sector　(62.B)　S.20.a.7.8.
   　　　　　　　Left Sector　(62.B)　S.1.d.6.1.

3. Routes of Evacuation.

   Right Sector. From forward Regimental Aid Post at point (62.B) S.16 central by Wheeled Stretchers cross country to relay post (62.B) S.20.a.7.8., thence by Wheeled Stretcher to Advanced Dressing Station SAVY. Walking cases follow the same route.

   From Advanced Dressing Station SAVY to FORESTE by the SAVY - ETREILLERS - GERMAINE Road.

   Left Sector. From forward Regimental Aid Post point (62.B) M.35.c.7.2. by FAYET - HOLNON Road to relay post (62.B) S.1.d.6.1., thence Stretcher Cases only by Car at night to FORESTE by the HOLNON - ATTILLY - ETREILLER - GERMAINE Road. Car reports departure at Advanced Dressing Station Left Sector & relief Car proceeds up to relay post.

3 continued.

Emergency cases (Abdominal etc) are to be brought across country by Wheeled Stretcher during day to Advanced Dressing Station, Left Sector, following cross country track, under cover, running between points (62.B) S.1.d.3.0. & (62.C) X.11.a.0.0.

Walking cases follow this same route to Advanced Dressing Station direct from relay post.

4. Cover for 30 patients (Stretcher Cases) is in process of erection at relay post (62.B) S.1.d.6.1.

5. All Regimental Aid Posts are provided with equipment as per your order 763M/17 para.2.

6. Each relay post & Regimental Aid Post is provided with 8 men & two Wheeled Stretcher Carriers.

7. The Advanced Dressing Station Left Sector, is under Capt. SCANLON with complete Section & equipment, two Cars & 1 Water Cart

The Advanced Dressing Station Right Sector, is under Capt. FISHER with complete Section & equipment, two Cars & 1 Water Cart.

8. A Horse Ambulance reports at each Advanced Dressing Station daily at 11.30 a.m., to collect the sick from the Battalions & Units in rest, on the return journey.

9. Constructional work is being pressed on.

Geo Thos Williamson

Lieut. Col. R.A.M.C.T.
O.C. 3rd. Field Ambulance.

2/5/17.

3rd. Field Ambulance.

APPENDIX VI

Unit.	17/5/17.		18/5/17.		21/5/17.		23/5/17.		Total.
	1.	2.	1.	2.	1.	2.	1.	2.	
2/8th. Worcs.	–	–	–	–	15	–	21	–	36
2/7th. Worcs.	1	4	8	–	6	–	7	–	26
2/6th. Glos.	5	–	4	–	4	–	–	–	13
2/4th. Glos.	1	–	4	–	13	–	10	–	28
183rd. M.G.C	8	–	–	–	9	–	7	–	24
183rd. T.M.B.	–	–	–	–	–	–	3	–	3
							TOTAL.		130

Sgd Geo Scott Williamson

Lieut.Col.R.A.M.C.T.
O.C. 2/3rd.S.M.Field Ambulance.

1. Cases carried from previous destination.
2. Cases picked up on the march.

CONFIDENTIAL   140/220

WAR DIARY

OF

2/3RD SOUTH MIDLAND FIELD AMBULANCE

FROM JUNE 1st 1917.   TO   JUNE 30TH 1917

(VOLUME ————)

COMMITTEE FOR THE
MEDICAL HISTORY OF THE WAR
Date 7 AUG. 1917

CONFIDENTIAL

140/298

WAR DIARY

OF

2/3RD SOUTH MIDLAND FIELD AMBULANCE

FROM July 1st 1917 TO July 31st 1917

(VOLUME   )

COMMITTEE FOR THE
MEDICAL HISTORY OF THE WAR
Date   10 SEP. 1917

B.E.F.

SUMMARY OF MEDICAL WAR DIARIES OF 2/3rd S.M.F.A.

<u>61st Div. 8th Corps. 5th ARMY.</u>
19th Corps from Aug. 15th.
5th Corps from Sept. 7th.
17th Corps. 3rd ARMY from 19th Sept.

<u>Western Front Operations</u> - "July - November 1917"

Officer Commanding - Lt.Col. G.Scott.Williamson.
Capt. C.L. Lander (T). to O.C. from 9th Sept.

SUMMARISED UNDER THE FOLLOWING HEADINGS:-

<u>Phase "D" 1. Passchendaele Operations, July-Nov.1917.</u>

(a) - Operations commencing 1/7/17.

(b) - Operations commencing 1/10/17.
    Canadians attacked Passchendaele, Oct. 30th.
    Canadians took Passchendaele, Nov.6th.

B.E.F.

1.

<u>2/3rd S.M.F.A. 61st Div. 8th Corps. 5th ARMY.</u> WESTERN FRONT.
<u>Officer Commanding - Lt.Col. G. Scott Williamson.</u> July-Aug. 1917.
<u>19th Corps from Aug. 15th.</u>

<u>PHASE "D" 1. Passchendaele Operations, July - Nov. 1917.</u>

   (a) - <u>Operations commencing 1/7/17.</u>

<u>Headquarters at PEENHOF.</u> B16. C. 5.5. Sheet 27.

July 26th.	<u>Moves.</u>) <u>Transfer.</u>)	Unit arrived in 8th Corps Area from 6th Corps. 1st ARMY.

B.E.F.

1.

2/3rd S.M.R.A. 61st Div. 8th Corps. 5th ARMY.   WESTERN FRONT.
                                                July-Aug. 1917.

Officer Commanding - Lt.Col. G. Scott Williamson.

19th Corps from Aug. 15th.

PHASE "D" 1.   Passchendaele Operations, July - Nov. 1917.

  (a) - Operations commencing 1/7/17.

Headquarters at PEENHOF. B16. C. 5.5. Sheet 27.

July 26th. Moves.   ) Unit arrived in 8th Corps Area from 6th Corps.
            Transfer.)
                        1st ARMY.

Army Form C. 2118.

WAR DIARY
or
INTELLIGENCE SUMMARY.
(Erase heading not required.)

MAP REFERENCES.
FRANCE. LENS 11 Sheet 1/100,000
BELGIUM HAZEBROUCK Sheet 5A 1/100,000
SHEET 27 BELGIUM - FRANCE

Place	Date	Hour	Summary of Events and Information	Remarks and references to Appendices
OEUF	JULY 1st		Field Ambulance training in Field Work & Disciplinary Parades. Capt. G.W. RIDGEWAY joined Unit	
	2nd		as above	
	3rd		as above	
	4th		as above. Capt TEASTOWELL joined Unit	
	5		as above	
	6th		as above. Capt. METCALFE left Unit for ENGLAND	
	7th		as above	map
	8		as above	
	9		as above	
	10		Staff tour with Lt Col BROUGH, explaining Tactical exercise	LENS 11 1/100,000
	11		as above	
	12		as above	
	13		Field Day with Regimental Medical Officers of the 183 BRIGADE.	
	14		Field Training & Physical exercise & Sports.	
	15		as above	
	16		as above	
	17		as above	
	18		as above	
	19		as above	
	20		as above	
	21		as above	
	22		as above	
	23		as above	
	24		as above	
	25		as above	
ZEGGERS CAPPEL	26		MOVE from OEUF to ZEGGERS CAPPEL by train from HOUVIN. Entrain at HOUVIN 1.49 a.m. Arrive ESQUELBECQ 10.15 a.m. March to PEENHOFF FARM. Map Ref SHEET 27 B16 c 5.5.	map HAZEBROUCK SHEET 5A 1/100,000
	27		Opened out under Canvas & Barns as a Divisional Rest Station. Two sections Field Training, one section as Rest Station.	
	28		as above	
	29		as above	
	30		as above	
	31		as above	

Geo John Williamson
Lt Col Comd 2/3 SM FD Amb

CONFIDENTIAL

WAR DIARY

OF

2/3rd SOUTH MIDLAND FIELD AMBULANCE

FROM August 1st 1917   TO August 31st 1917

(VOLUME   )

COMMITTEE FOR THE
MEDICAL HISTORY OF THE WAR
Date -1 OCT. 1917

B.E.F.

SUMMARY OF MEDICAL WAR DIARIES OF 2/3rd S.M.F.A.

61st Div. 8th Corps. 5th ARMY.

19th Corps from Aug. 15th.

5th Corps from Sept. 7th.

17th Corps. 3rd ARMY from 19th Sept.

Western Front Operations - "July - November 1917"

Officer Commanding - Lt.Col. G. Scott Williamson.
Capt. C.L. Lander (T). to O.C. from 9th Sept.

SUMMARISED UNDER THE FOLLOWING HEADINGS:-

Phase "D" 1. Passchendaele Operations, July-Nov.1917.

(a) - Operations commencing 1/7/17.

(b) - Operations commencing 1/10/17.
Canadians attacked Passchendaele, Oct. 30th.
Canadians took Passchendaele, Nov. 6th.

AUGUST.
1st-14th.   Operations R.A.M.C. Routine and Training.
15th.   Moves.) Unit transferred with 61st Division to 19th
        Transfer.) Corps and moved to MILL FARM L. 13.d.3.2. (Sheet
        27).

B.E.F.

2/3rd S.M.F.A. 61st Div. 19th Corps. 5th ARMY. WESTERN FRONT.
August 1917
Officer Commanding - Lt.Col. G. Scott Williamson.

PHASE "D" 1. Passchendaele Operations, July-Nov.1917.
(a) - Operations commencing 1/7/17.

Headquarters at MILL FARM, L.13.d.3.2. Sheet 27.

Aug. 15th. Moves.) Unit transferred with 61st Division to 18th
Transfer.) Corps and moved to MILL FARM L.13.d.3.2.
(Sheet 27).

17th. Moves. To WIELTJE, C.28.a.9.5. (Sheet 28).

Medical Arrangements. A.D.S. taken over from 109th F.A.
R.A.P's at RAT FARM (L), PLUM FARM (R).
2 Col. P's formed at DEAD END CANAL
BANK and St. JEAN. 50 bearers 2/1st S.M.F.A. and 34
bearers 2/2nd S.M.F.A. joined for duty.

Unit collected wounded from Line.

Assistance. Unit augmented by Stretcher Bearers from Infantry
Battalions not in line.

Evacuation. By hand from R.A.P's to A.D.S. over ground
continually searched by enemy fire. W.W. by lorries and
charabancs from A.D.S. to C.W.W.C.P. at VLAMERTINGHE MILL.
S.W. by cars to C.M.D.S. RED FARM and C.C.S. REMY SIDING.

25th. Medical Arrangements.) R.A.P. moved from RAT FARM to
Ops. Enemy.) SPREE FARM C18.d.2.3. owing to
constant direct fire of enemy.

Casualties R.A.M.C. Capt. Coleman attached 2/6th Glosters
wounded.

28th. Capt. Cornelius attached 2/8th
Worcesters wounded.

B.E.F.

2/3rd S.M.F.A. 61st Div. 19th Corps. 5th ARMY.

Officer Commanding - Lt.Col. Scott)   WESTERN FRONT.
                                Williamson.)   Aug.-Sept.1917.

5th Corps from Sept. 7th.

PHASE "D" 1. Passchendaele Operations, July-Nov. 1917.
    (a) - Operations commencing 1/7/17.

Aug. 30th.	Casualties R.A.M.C. Lt.Col. Scott-Williamson and 14 bearers missing - believed captured while collecting wounded from front line - No firing heard at the time.
Sept. 7th.	Transfer. Unit transferred with 61st Div. to 5th Corps.

B.E.F.

2/3rd (S.M. F.A. 61st Div. 19th Corps. 5th ARMY. WESTERN FRONT
Officer Commanding -Lt.Col. G. Scott. Williamson.
Aug. 1917.

PHASE "D" 1. Passchendaele Operations, July-Nov.1917.
  (a) - Operations commencing 1/7/17.

Headquarters at MILL FARM, L.13.d.3.2. Sheet 27.

Aug. 15th. Moves.) Unit transferred with 61st Division to 19th
    Transfer.)
      Corps and moved to MILL FARM L.13.d.3.2.
(Sheet 27).

17th. Moves. To WIELTJE, C.28.a.9.5. (Sheet 28).

Medical Arrangements. A.D.S. taken over from 109th F.A.
    R.A.P's at RAT FARM (L) PHUM FARM (R).
    2 Col. P's formed at DEAD END CANAL
BANK and St. JEAN. 50 bearers 2/1st S.M. F.A. and 34
bearers 2/2nd S.M.F.A. joined for duty.
Unit collected wounded from Line.
Assistance. Unit augmented by Stretcher Bearers from Infantry
Battalions not in line.
Evacuation. By hand from R.A.P's to A.D.S. over ground
continually searched by enemy fire. W.W. by lorries and
charabancs from A.D.S. to C.W.W.C.P. at VLAMERTINGHE MILL.
S.W. by cars to C.M.D.S. RED FARM and C.C.S. REMY SIDING.

25th. Medical Arrangements.) R.A.P. moved from RAT FARM to
   Ops. Enemy.   )
      SPREE FARM C18.d.2.3. owing to
constant direct fire of enemy.
Casualties R.A.M.C. Capt. Coleman attached 2/6th Glosters
    wounded.

28th.   Capt Cornelius attached 2/8th
Worcesters wounded.

B.E.F.

2/3rd (S.M) F.A. 61st Div. 19th Corps. 5th ARMY.

Officer Commanding - Lt.Col. Scott)   WESTERN FRONT.
                                  Williamson.)   Aug.-Sept. 1917.

5th Corps from Sept. 7th.

PHASE "D" 1. Passchendaele Operations, July-Nov. 1917.
    (a) - Operations commencing 1/7/17.

Aug. 30th.	Casualties R.A.M.C. Lt.Col. Scott-Williamson and 14 bearers missing - believed captured while collecting wounded from front line - No firing heard at the time.
Sept. 7th.	Transfer. Unit transferred with 61st Div. to 5th Corps.

AUGUST.
1st-14th.   Operations R.A.M.C. Routine and Training.

15th.   Moves.   ) Unit transferred with 61st Division to 10th
        Transfer.)
                      Corps and moved to MILL FARM L. 13.d.3.2. (Sheet 27).

Army Form C. 2118.

WAR DIARY
or
INTELLIGENCE SUMMARY.
(Erase heading not required.)

Place	Date	Hour	Summary of Events and Information	Remarks and references to Appendices
PEEN HOFF FARM	Aug 1.		Routine duties & Hospital duties carried on. A batch of 3. men were sent on several occasions to assist the former, weed clearing etc.	WWW WWW
"	7.		A Brigade practice attack was practised. The Ambulance moved out with the 1st advanced division and learned intercommunication necessary with the Brigade Ambulance and transport. A suitable site was selected and an A.D.S. formed. The bye bearer subdivisions went forward under three officers + maintained touch with the right + left Battalion M.O.s. W/c the advance relay posts were found with the stretcher squads under a subordinate M.O. The practice was instructive + worked well.	WWW WWW WWW WWW WWW WWW
"	14		Routine duties carried on during the week. Practice with the box respirators + frequent instruction in gas attacks with special reference to the new lachrymator shell.	WWW WWW WWW
MILL FARM I 28 d 3.4 Map 2.1	Aug 16		Ambulance entrained to POPERINGE and marched to MILL FARM. Transport by road. Bivouaced for one night.	WWW WWW

Army Form C. 2118.

WAR DIARY
or
INTELLIGENCE SUMMARY.
(Erase heading not required.)

Place	Date	Hour	Summary of Events and Information	Remarks and references to Appendices
GOLDFISH CHATEAU	Aug 17		Marched from MILLFARM to GOLDFISH CHATEAU. Transport bivouacked to the right. Lt Col. Scott Williamson, Capt Scanlan and Lieut.	
H.Q. D.2.C.	Aug 28		RIDGEWAY proceeded with 70 bearers to A.D.S. WIGETSE and took 60 on from 101 F.Amb. Two explosions of heaves, 50 men from 2/1st F.Amb and 54 from 3/1st F.Amb. were attached to A.D.S. placing a series of pillboxes + mine shafts which are lighted by electric light. These pillboxes + mine shafts run at a depth of 25 to 80 feet below the ground. They are used [illegible] but very unconfortable. Dugouts for the left contain a struck to help the invalid. The stretcher cases go down a [illegible] flights at the entrance along a railway incline that the lower levels second incline [illegible] the entrance which is fairly. Three [illegible] traffic were also here. Prisoners stretcher cases the time. The walking wounded use staircases from the lower entrance + evacuated with transport so the care. Space was felt before leaving to fill up [illegible] time to	

WAR DIARY
or
INTELLIGENCE SUMMARY.

Army Form C. 2118.

Place	Date	Hour	Summary of Events and Information	Remarks and references to Appendices
WIELTJE ADS	Red 17		Reconnoitred cross routes for allotment for attention in the first instance cases waiting for evacuation in the second. Proceeded in Kitchener's Wood by car to Corps Main Dressing Station at Red Farm or CCS at Brandhoek. Owing to being shelled the latter had to chiefly cases evacuated to REMY SIDING. A car carrying wounded at DEAD END CANAL BANK caught of 15 DAIMLER AMBULANCES and 2 FORD cars. These latter very useful for special cases of chemical wounds + that sort of special difficulty. Wounded were evacuated as as to to CRS's working wounded 'best walking cases + stretcher' to CCR's. Working wounded 'lost' also made of VLAMERTINGHE MILL. On Spoord occasion were also made of the walking wounded way from WADS (now ST JEAN to WIELTJE (both the local cases and cases from END WCQ CANAL BANK and ST JEAN. These finally carried by an MOO to were in the future tense the RAPS were at WHITWM to the left route, and PLUM FARM to the right a less Base.	

WAR DIARY
or
INTELLIGENCE SUMMARY.

Army Form C. 2118.

Place	Date	Hour	Summary of Events and Information	Remarks and references to Appendices
	Aug		[illegible handwritten entry spanning multiple lines, approximately:] ...attack... the field ambulance formed and ... by hand ... to the A.D.S. about 1 mile. Two R.A.M.C. runners were kept with each Regimental M.O. for communication with the A.D.S. Owing to the heavy shelling... of the found squads consisted of six men. The field Ambulance bearers were ... augmented by auxiliary stretcher bearers taken from the Battalions within the line. The carrying was often done under shell fire which continually fouled the stretcher bearers.	
Wieltje ADS	Aug 16		Capt COLEMAN R.A.M.C. att. 2/6 GLOUCESTERS reconnoitred the area in company of O.C. ADS WIELTJE last night + this 4 + this M... the occurrence of RAT FARM c.18.d.2.3 (FREZENBERG MAP) and his R.A.P. to SPREE FARM c.18.d.16 was unten-able owing to constant direct fire. Capt COLEMAN was slightly wounded thus without any carried on his duties [illegible] believed the following day	

Army Form C. 2118.

WAR DIARY
or
INTELLIGENCE SUMMARY.
(Erase heading not required.)

Instructions regarding War Diaries and Intelligence Summaries are contained in F. S. Regs., Part II. and the Staff Manual respectively. Title pages will be prepared in manuscript.

Place	Date	Hour	Summary of Events and Information	Remarks and references to Appendices
WIETJE	Aug 28		CAPT CORNELIUS R.A.M.C. att 2/8 R. WORCESTERS was slightly wounded but remained on duty until relief the following day, when he was evacuated to the C.C.S.	WW
			D.C. 2/3 SM&FM&B	WW
	29		Lt. Col. SCOTT WILLIAMSON took a party of stretcher bearers up to the front line and cleared it and the ground in front of wounded men lying in shell holes. Capt WOOD R.A.M.C.T. assisted. There was no firing on any of the parties.	WW WW WW WW
	30		Lt. Col. SCOTT WILLIAMSON again took a party of stretcher bearers, leaving the A.D.S. at 6.45 a.m. Four squads of bearers, hire of the bearers were not back with casualties from the front line. The remainder 16 in number & Lt SCOTT WILLIAMSON did not return and no information, except that parties of bearers were seen moving about beyond AISNE HOUSE, about 10.30 a.m., has been received as to their movements.	WW WW WW WW WW WW

Army Form C. 2118.

WAR DIARY
or
INTELLIGENCE SUMMARY.
(Erase heading not required.)

Place	Date	Hour	Summary of Events and Information	Remarks and references to Appendices
WIELTJE ADS	Aug 31.		No word as of the missing party has come in. No prisoners have been during the previous morning and it is presumed that the whole party have been taken prisoner. In consequence of Lt Scott-Williamson being missing, notes & matters of interest in the diary have not been available.	WW WW WW WW WW

W. Vincent Wood
Capt R.A.M.C. T.
O/c Oct 2/6 S.M. Amb.

MEDICAL

CONFIDENTIAL

WAR DIARY

OF

2/3RD SOUTH MIDLAND FIELD AMBULANCE

FROM SEPTEMBER 1st 1917   TO SEPTEMBER 30TH 1917

(VOLUME _____)

COMMITTEE FOR THE
MEDICAL HISTORY OF THE WAR
Date -5 NOV. 1917

B.E.F.

2/3rd (S.M) F.A.   61st Div. 5th Corps. 5th ARMY. WESTERN FRONT.
Officer Commanding - Lt.Col. G.Scott Williamson.
Sept.1917.

Capt. C.L.Lander (T) to O.C. from 9th Sept.
17th Corps. 3rd ARMY from 18th Sept.

PHASE "D" 1. Passchendaele Operations,"July - Nov. 1917."

(a) - Operations commencing 1/7/17.

At WIELTJE, C.28.a.9.5. (Sheet 28).

Sept. 7th. Transfer. Unit transferred with 61st Div. to 5th Corps.
Casualties R.A.M.C. O & 2 killed. O & 3 wounded while bringing wounded from PLUM FARM to A.D.S.

9th. Appointment. Capt./C.L. Lander (T) to Officer Commanding 2/3rd S.M.F.A. vice Lt.Col. Scott Williamson missing.

10th. Operations Enemy, Gas.   ) Area round A.D.S. shelled with
Casualties. Gas.   )
Casualties R.A.M.C, Gas.   ) mustard gas shells. Large number of R.F.A. evacuated.
Casualties R.A.M.C, Gas. O & 49 gassed.

13th. Casualties R.A.M.C. Capt. Jones Evans died of wounds.

14th. Medical Arrangements. A.D.S. and forward posts handed over to 2/1st W. Lancs F.A.

15th. Moves. To L.19.b.3.8. (Sheet 27).

18th. Moves.   ) Unit transferred with 61st Div. to 17th Corps
Transfer.)   3rd ARMY and moved to ARRAS.

B.E.F.

<u>2/3rd S.M.F.A. 61st Div. 5th Corps. 5th ARMY.</u> WESTERN FRONT.

<u>Officer Commanding - Lt.Col. G. Scott Williamson.</u>

Sept. 1917.

<u>Capt. C.L. Lander (T) to O.C. from 9th Sept.</u>
<u>17th Corps. 3rd ARMY from 18th Sept.</u>

<u>PHASE "D" 1. Passchendaele Operations,"July - Nov. 1917."</u>

(a) - <u>Operations commencing 1/7/17.</u>

At WIELTJE, C.28.a.9.5. (Sheet 28).

Sept. 7th. <u>Transfer.</u> Unit transferred with 61st Div. to 5th Corps.

<u>Casualties R.A.M.C.</u> O & 2 killed. O & 3 wounded while bringing wounded from PLUM FARM to A.D.S.

9th. <u>Appointment.</u> Capt. C.L. Lander (T) to Officer Commanding 2/3rd S.M.F.A. vice Lt.Col. Scott Williamson missing.

10th. <u>Operations Enemy, Gas.</u>) Area round A.D.S. shelled with
<u>Casualties. Gas.</u>)
<u>Casualties R.A.M.C, Gas.</u>) mustard gas shells. Large number of R.F.A. evacuated.

<u>Casualties R.A.M.C, Gas.</u> O & 49 gassed.

13th. <u>Casualties R.A.M.C.</u> Capt. Jones Evans died of wounds.

14th. <u>Medical Arrangements.</u> A.D.S. and forward posts handed over to 2/1st W. Lancs F.A.

15th. <u>Moves.</u> To L.19.b.3.8. (Sheet 27).

18th. <u>Moves.</u>   ) Unit transferred with 61st Div. to 17th Corps
<u>Transfer.</u>) 3rd ARMY and moved to ARRAS.

Army Form C. 2118.

WAR DIARY
or
INTELLIGENCE SUMMARY.
(Erase heading not required.)

Instructions regarding War Diaries and Intelligence Summaries are contained in F. S. Regs., Part II. and the Staff Manual respectively. Title pages will be prepared in manuscript.

Place	Date	Hour	Summary of Events and Information	Remarks and references to Appendices
WIELTJE MINE SHAFT ADS	Sept. 1st		Capt. PEMBERTON. RAMC and DALE WOOD RAMC reported for duty. Visited the Q.M. stores at RIDGE CAMP, and also the car park at RED FARM. C.M.D.S. Water supplies and medical stores supply working satisfactorily.	
	2.		Capt. RIDGWAY of the unit temporarily attached for duty to 2/6 12. WARWICKS.	
	6.		Capt. RIDGWAY evacuated sick and replaced by Capt SPEEDY GRIFFITHS. Capt SPEEDY relieved Capt PEMBERTON. ADMS visited ADS, and walked up towards PLUM FARM to see condition of line of evacuation.	
	7.		One squad of bearers knocked out by a shell while bringing a case down from PLUM FARM RAP. Two killed and three wounded. Patient escaped without further injury.	

Army Form C. 2118.

WAR DIARY
or
INTELLIGENCE SUMMARY.
(Erase heading not required.)

Instructions regarding War Diaries and Intelligence Summaries are contained in F. S. Regs., Part II. and the Staff Manual respectively. Title pages will be prepared in manuscript.

Place	Date	Hour	Summary of Events and Information	Remarks and references to Appendices
WIELTJE A.D.S. C28c95 Sheet 28	Sept 9		Capt. SPEEDY detailed to 2/5 GLOUCESTERS to relieve Capt. C. LLANDER RAMC. who assumed command of the Ambulance	C.W.
	10		A mustard gas shell exploded in the trench at main entrance to advanced dressing station at WIELTJE in the afternoon, small quantities of gas travelled into the mine shaft continuously afterwards	C.W. C.W. C.W. C.W.
	11		Early in the morning the effects of the gas were manifest in the occupants of the Dressing Rooms. 22 men of the Ambulance were evacuated to the Corps MAIN DRESSING at RED FARM. 16 slight cases were sent to rest at CANAL BANK. The most marked symptoms of all these cases was conjunctivitis with ædema of the eye-lids from same cause.	C.W. C.W. C.W. C.W. C.W.
			A large number of casualties from gas amongst the R.F.A. evacuated from the area near WIELTJE.	C.W. C.W. C.W.
			Cpl. WIDMANN and 8 men were evacuated from the POST at ST JEAN from same cause	C.W. C.W.
	13	8.30 p.m.	Capt. SCANLON RAMC, on duty at WIELTJE, having received a message that Capt. JONES EVANS RAMC had been wounded at SPREE FARM, proceeded to his relief with a party of stretcher bearers. The bearers returned with Capt JONES EVANS	C.W. C.W. C.W.

WAR DIARY
or
INTELLIGENCE SUMMARY.

Army Form C. 2118.

Place	Date	Hour	Summary of Events and Information	Remarks and references to Appendices
WIELTJE A.D.S. C28 a 95 Sh. 28	Sept. 13		Who died at the advanced dressing station at 8.20 p.m. Capt. SCANLON remained on duty at SPREE FARM until relieved by Capt. BERRY RAMC ⅔ 2/4 R. BERKS.	C.H.L C.H.L
	14		The slight gas cases of the ambulance sent for rest to CANAL BANK evacuated to CORPS REST STATION at HILLHOEK.	C.H.L C.H.L
			The ambulance was relieved by the 2/1 WEST LANCASHIRE FIELD AMBULANCE and left CANAL BANK for the transport lines at RIDGE CAMP. A party of NCOs+men under	C.H.L P.H.L C.H.L
WATOU No 2 Area L.9.f.38 Sh. 27	15		Capt. SCANLON remained at WIELTJE A.D.S. until the relief was complete. The rear party reported but. The transport marched under 184 Brigade orders to WATOU No 2 Area (L.9.f.38 Sh.27). The personnel entrained under 184 Brigade orders at VLAMERTINGHE and joined the transport in a Canvas Camp at L.9.f.38 Sh.27.	C.H.L C.H.L C.H.L
Le Nouveau Monde I.17.a Sh.27	16		Capt. ROBSON attached + detailed for duty with the D.A.C. the same day.	C.H.L C.H.L
	17		Marched with 163 Brigade to billets at Le NOUVEAU MONDE. I.17.a.9.5 Sh. 27 WORMHOUDT area Capt. GOMPERTZ RAMC returned from 64 C.C.S. PROVEN with 22 men, paraded detached.	C.H.L C.H.L
	18		Capt. GOMPERTZ detailed for 24 hours duty at BAVINCHOVE Station CASSEL during entraining of 163 Brigade. Capt. SCANLON detailed for a similar period during detrainment at ARRAS.	C.H.L C.H.L

WAR DIARY
or
INTELLIGENCE SUMMARY.

(Erase heading not required.)

Army Form C. 2118.

Place	Date	Hour	Summary of Events and Information	Remarks and references to Appendices
LE NOUVEAU MONDE	Sept 19		Marched to BAVINCHOVE Stn. "CASSEL" 01/6 A F.O. Sheet 27. Entrained at 8.31 a.m. for ARRAS	Ch/
IIIA Sheet 27			Arrived ARRAS 2.15 p.m. detrained without mishap marched to camp previously occupied by unit at SIMENCOURT Q.10. Sheet 51C. Hospital opened for sick of 153rd Brigade.	Ch/ Ch/
SIMENCOURT Q.10 Sheet 51C	20		Capt GOMPERTZ R.A.M.C. + 1 nursing orderly detached for duty to XVII Corps School of Musketry + Reinforcement Camp at SAVY	Ch/ Ch/
			Lt. CROOM reported for duty and detached to XVII Corps Rest Station at WARLUS	Ch/
ARRAS G.22.b.6.3 Sheet 51.B	21		One tent subdivision detached for duty at No. 19 C.C.S. Four men detached for water duty to No. 51 Sanitary Section and one clerk to XVII Corps Rest Station.	Ch/ Ch/
			Marched to ARRAS and took over Divisional Main Dressing Station at HOSPICE de VIEILLARDS with transport lines at DEAD MANS CORNER from 52nd Field Ambulance	Ch/
			Relief completed at midnight	Ch/
	22		Prepared hospital to receive up to 100 patients	Ch/ Ch/
	24		Lt. THORNHILL U.S.M.S. taken on strength + attached to XVII C.R.S. WARLUS	Ch/
			to replace Lt. CROOM sick.	Ch/
	25		Improving hospital buildings, preparing house adjoining HOSPICE as hospital	Ch/

Army Form C. 2118.

WAR DIARY
or
INTELLIGENCE SUMMARY.
(Erase heading not required.)

Instructions regarding War Diaries and Intelligence Summaries are contained in F. S. Regs., Part II. and the Staff Manual respectively. Title pages will be prepared in manuscript.

Place	Date	Hour	Summary of Events and Information	Remarks and references to Appendices
ARRAS G22 O.2. 51st S.I.B	Sept 25		to Officers, preparing accomodation for treatment of scabies	Ch.
	26		Continuing above preparations	Ch.
			Officers hospital to accomodate 8 completed	Ch.
	30		Capt C.J. HEVER & Capt H.B STONE - U.S.M.S. posted for instruction	Ch.

Chlarler
Capt RAMC
O/c 2/3 S. Midland Field Ambulance

Medical /VC/18

CONFIDENTIAL 40/2499

WAR DIARY.

OF

2/3RD. SOUTH MIDLAND FIELD AMBULANCE

FROM. OCTOBER 1ST. 1917   TO. OCTOBER 31ST. 1917

(VOLUME   )

COMMITTEE FOR THE
MEDICAL HISTORY OF THE WAR
Date -8 DEC. 1917

Army Form C. 2118.

WAR DIARY
or
INTELLIGENCE SUMMARY.
(Erase heading not required.)

Instructions regarding War Diaries and Intelligence Summaries are contained in F. S. Regs., Part II. and the Staff Manual respectively. Title pages will be prepared in manuscript.

Place	Date	Hour	Summary of Events and Information	Remarks and references to Appendices
ARRAS	Oct 1		Routine duties, inspecting hospital. Capt GREEN conducted Capts STONE and HEVER USMS	CdL
	2.		to the A.D.S. on right sector of divisional front	CdL
			The Ambulance hospital visited by an officer from the Russian Embassy Paris. Routine duties	CdL
			100 beds occupied in hospital. Lt Col BURROUGHES took USA officers on left sector of the line.	CdL
	3		House in Rue de CROISSART opened as a hospital for officers	CdL
	5		Routine duties	CdL
	6		Capts STONE & HEVER accompanied O/c to visit WIELTJE district near YPRES	CdL
	7		Capt HALLET R.A.M.C. reported for duty	4/A
	8		Routine duties. In priory hospital & Garden planted with vegetables. Detachment from French A. Ench.	dL
			in ARRAS.	dL
	9		Capts STONE & HEVER U.S.M.C. left for No 19 C.C.S. Capt C LANDER proceeded on	dL
			leave & handed over command of the Ambulance to Capt. W.Y. WOOD.	CdL
	10		Routine duties.	
	11.		Visit by D.D.M.S.	WWW
	12.		Structural alterations and improvement in accommodation well forward	WWW

WAR DIARY
or
INTELLIGENCE SUMMARY.
(Erase heading not required.)

Army Form C. 2118.

Instructions regarding War Diaries and Intelligence Summaries are contained in F. S. Regs., Part II. and the Staff Manual respectively. Title pages will be prepared in manuscript.

Place	Date	Hour	Summary of Events and Information	Remarks and references to Appendices
ARRAS	Dec. 15.		Arrone winder Hospitals accommodation 30 to 90, mainly P.U.O. cases. Paper was	
			being used in mattress making, a very satisfactory substitute.	
			Boxing ring erected in a spare room for the use of the men.	
	18.		Visit of DMS and DDMS. DMS approved of the present arrangements + working.	
	20		The officer in charge of Engineers went round + arranged for the repair of roofs	
			of main hospital & the future hand advance. Lt's CHRAPE, LISTON + KNOTT reported reported (arrival)	
			Lt Col. Lauder returned from leave & resumed command.	
	21.		Capt. SCANLON detailed for duty with 2/1 Bucks Bett: and struck off the strength of the Ambulance	
			Instructions received to increase hospital accommodation to 150 beds.	
	22			
	24		S. Luir detailed for 48 hrs duty with 2/1 S. Midland Field Ambulance.	
			RE's in readiness to roof in the Hospice W. of the Chapel	
	27		Lt. ARNOTT attached temporarily for duty with 226 Bde. R.F.A.	
	28		Capt. WOOD went on leave.	
	29		Routine duties and improvement to premises.	
	31		All NCOs + men of this field Ambulance examined + classified in Categories A. + B.	
			Lt.Col. SHAW & Major R.E. MACDONALD V.S.M.C. reported for one week's instruction.	

O/c 2/3 S. Midland Field Amb.

CONFIDENTIAL
WAR DIARY
OF
2/3RD SOUTH MIDLAND FIELD AMBULANCE

From 1st November 1917   To 30th November 1917

(VOLUME _____)

COMMITTEE FOR THE
MEDICAL HISTORY OF THE WAR
Date 17 JAN. 1918

Army Form C. 2118.

WAR DIARY
or
INTELLIGENCE SUMMARY.
(Erase heading not required.)

Instructions regarding War Diaries and Intelligence Summaries are contained in F.S. Regs., Part II and the Staff Manual respectively. Title pages will be prepared in manuscript.

Place	Date	Hour	Summary of Events and Information	Remarks and references to Appendices
ARRAS Sheet 51.B G.22.4.03.	Nov 1		G.O.C. the Division presented acting Lance Corporal DEWFALL with a parchment for gallantry.	Chr
	2		Capt. BISHOP returned from leave.	Chr
	3		Lieut CHAPPLE left the ambulance for duty at No 5 C.C.S. R.E.s completed roof of west wing. & Capt. Bishop made officer in charge of wards.	Chr Chr
	5		Additional wards opened, no patients during day. Iell. Two small pigs purchased at 950L market.	Chr Chr
	6		Hospital visited by DDMS XVII Corps + ADMS 61st Div.	Chr
	7		Col. SHAW and Major MACDONALD visited front areas with Capt. MAY. Lecture to gas helpers given	Chr
	8		Col. SHAW and Major MACDONALD left for instruction at No 20 C.C.S. BOISLEUX by the III Army School of Cookery	Chr
	9		Eight reinforcements arrived. Hand stacking under cover completed at transport lines.	Chr
	11		Arrangements completed for testing the efficiency of all patients on admission to hospital.	Chr
	12		Work of cleaning out decontaminating hospital and officers wards proceeded with.	Chr
			A man drew chipped and cook's boiler flooded with water. Drain cleared by pumps and after considerable excavation a burst main be discovered & emptied.	Chr Chr
	13		Two reinforcements arrived.	Chr
	14		Proceeding with routine duties. No of patients in hospital increased to 175. A consignment of 80 frozen chicken received as medical comforts for sick.	Chr Chr
	17		Lieut. LISTON q m o O.R. proceeded to ALBERT to inspect III Army School of Cooking.	Chr

Army Form C. 2118.

WAR DIARY
or
INTELLIGENCE SUMMARY.
(Erase heading not required.)

Army Form C. 2118.

Instructions regarding War Diaries and Intelligence Summaries are contained in F. S. Regs., Part II. and the Staff Manual respectively. Title pages will be prepared in manuscript.

Place	Date	Hour	Summary of Events and Information	Remarks and references to Appendices
ARRAS Sheet 51B G 26 b 03	Nov. 18		Lieut. ARIOTT and nine men detailed for temporary duty at No 29 C.C.S.	Cpl
	19		Conference of O's.C. Field Ambulances at Office of A.D.M.S. to arrange R.A.M.C. dispositions in the event of German retirement on this front.	Cpl
	22		Routine duties of hospital.	Cpl
	24		Heavy gale of wind during the night causing considerable damage to roof of hospital & to the roof of house used as hospital for officers.	Cpl Cpl Cpl
	25		Lieut. THORNHILL M.O.R.C. reported for duty from XVII C.R.S. in relief of Capt. BOLSTER R.A.M.C. of 2/2 S. Midland Field Ambulance	Cpl Cpl
	26		Notified by A.D.M.S. that Capt. BOLSTER L.E. and Lieut W.L.M.DAY R.A.M.C. were placed on the strength of this unit and were doing detached duty at XVII C.R.S & No 19 C.C.S. respectively. Lt. + Q.M. S.BROOKES acted as prisoners friend in a Court Martial held at this hospital on Pte. GRIMES 18th M.G.C. who was acquitted.	Cpl Cpl Cpl
	27		Capt. BISHOP R.A.M.C. having been granted leave proceeded to PARIS. Warning order of impending move received.	Cpl Cpl
	28		Patients evacuated from Hospital as follows 47 to duty, 52 to C.R.S, 27 to C.C.S. and 34 Convalescent patients were sent to the Divisional Depot Batt. at AGNEZ-le-DUISANS under	Cpl

WAR DIARY
or
INTELLIGENCE SUMMARY.
(Erase heading not required.)

Army Form C. 2118.

Mob. Sher 51A

Place	Date	Hour	Summary of Events and Information	Remarks and references to Appendices
ARRAS G 22 B 03	Nov 28		The care of Lieut THORNHILL M.O.R.R and 4 O.R. This Offr was taken under instructions from A.D.M.S. to avoid excessive evacuation when moving. Capt BOLSTER reported for duty.	AAA
	29		Remaining patient in Hospital evacuated as follows; to duty 3, to C.R.S. 20, to C.C.S. 30 to Div Dep't Bath 17. Hospital completely evacuated & closed. All excess of medical stores returned to Advanced Depot of Med. Stores. Red Cross Stores returned to B.R.C.S. Instructions received to hand over the remaining Corps Stores taken on charge to the 45th FIELD AMBULANCE. ARRAS shelled by enemy.	AAA
	30		ARRAS reported foggy. Lieut DAY reported for duty. Pigs sold. All equipment checked, packed on wagons. Orders received to move to BARASTRE on the 30th to leave ARRAS by tram at 9.0 a.m. Orders altered at 3.0 a.m. to entrain at DAINVILLE instead of ARRAS. Unit moved off at 6.30 a.m. detrained at 8.30 a.m. Transport moved off under Capt WOOD & Lieut BROOKES at 7.30 a.m. & marched with brigaded transport. Lt. LISON attended at Entrainment. Lieut DAY at detrainment of Bde. Group 183. After detrainment of unit at BAPAUME when on the march to BARASTRE. Bde halted & after a interval unit embussed & proceeded to ROYAUCOURT thereafter marching to HAVRINCOURT WOOD map reference Q 15 a 7.5. Sheet 57c where the unit bivouacked with the 183 Bde Group. Transport bivouacked at ROYAUL COURT.	AAA
HAVRINCOURT WOOD Q15 a 7.5 Sheet 57c				

CH Hands Lt Col RAMC

CONFIDENTIAL

WAR DIARY.

OF

2/3rd SOUTH MIDLAND FIELD AMBULANCE

FROM December 1st. 1917   To December 31st. 1917

(VOLUME   )

COMMITTEE FOR THE
MEDICAL HISTORY OF THE WAR
Date −1 FEB. 1918

Army Form C. 2118.

MAPS. SHEET 57c.
17

WAR DIARY
or
INTELLIGENCE SUMMARY.
(Erase heading not required.)

Place	Date	Hour	Summary of Events and Information	Remarks and references to Appendices
HAVRINCOURT WOOD Q.13.d.	Dec. 1		Ambulance moved to METZ Q20a Sheet 57c. Transport rejoined Lieut P.S.L. LISTON R.A.M.C. evacuated to C.C.S.	CM
SH57c. METZ Q20. Sheet 57c.	2		Relieved 66th Field Ambulance at the A.D.S. at the sunken road between BEAUCAMP and VILLERS-PLOUICH R13.a.0.5. Sheet 57c. Capt MOORE R.A.M.C. and Lieut [illegible] 2/2nd 2nd/3rd S.Midfield Ambulance and Lieut PETERSEN + SANFORD MORE VSA & the 2/1Smithfield Amb. attached to details. Lieut GARRISON M.O.R.C. USA. Capt WOOD and SANFORD and 78 O.R. intelld. at A.D.S. Relay post at sunken road near CHARING CROSS Cala Q.17.6.19. Capt MOORE, Lieut PETERSEN and 20 O.R. in charge. Forty bearers sent to forward bearer post SURREY RAVINE R8.c.5. Mode of evacuation by horse ambulances from A.D.S. to TRESCAULT with relay post at CHARING CROSS. From TRESCAULT by motor ambulances and lorries to C.C.S. at YTRES. stretcher cases and C.M.D.S. FINS sick and walking wounded. Lieut ERICKSEN detailed for duty with 2/7 WORCESTERS.	CM
	3		Considerable difficulty in evacuation of wounded owing to trouble in locating Regtl Aid Post and the very bad state of the roads. (Horsed Ambulances removed & Ford Cars substituted in November.	CM

Army Form C. 2118.

WAR DIARY
or
INTELLIGENCE SUMMARY.
(Erase heading not required.)

Place	Date	Hour	Summary of Events and Information	Remarks and references to Appendices
METZ Q20 SW5ᵗ	Dec 3		Large Ambulances evacuated from as far forward as CHARING CROSS Cntr. New forward bearer post established at V8.b.3.7. Sgt Brunn and 40 S.Bearers installed to evacuate from R.A.P, a left divisional post line.	
FINS V19.a.9.1 SW5ᵗ			50 O.R. of 2/2 Field Ambulance and 4th (2/1)ˢᵗ attached for duty. also Ambulance Regimental S.Bs. Headquarter transport moved from METZ to FINS taken on billets from 6th Fd Amb. Motor Ambulances attached from 2/1 + 2/2 2ⁿᵈ Ambulance and from 46ᵗʰ M.A.C and from 4 lorries for walking wounded to evacuate wounded sick.	
	4		Capt. BISHOP R.A.M.C came up to A.D.S having returned from leave at PARIS. 1 cas DAY came reported for duty to 2/1 Field Amb. Auxiliary Stretcher Bearers still required as in medic.	Ok
	5		H.Q. at FINS shelled. L/Cpl Walker + Pte Hockbull Killed. #Cpl Pidgen wounded also two N.C.O.s of the Guards Killed. One G.S. Waggon destroyed + one Water cart damaged. Capt BISHOP detailed for duty with 2/6 GLOUCESTERS Capt UNDERHILL of 109 Fd. Amb. a 56 O.R. took over bearer post at V8.b.3.7 shot 6/C. on the relief of 182 Bde by 36ᵗʰ Division. Two 2ⁿᵈ Cars provided by 36ᵗʰ Divⁿ for work in forward area.	Ok Ok
V11.b.4.4. SW.5ᵗ	6		Capt. WOOD moved H.Q. Transport W of FINS to V11.b.44 on account of shelling at FINS leaving bearing party. Auxiliary S.Bs. still required	Ok Ok

WAR DIARY or INTELLIGENCE SUMMARY

Army Form C. 2118.

Place	Date	Hour	Summary of Events and Information	Remarks and references to Appendices
VILLERS	Dec. 7		Lt. DAY R.A.M.C. evacuated to 2/1st H.Amb. F.C.C.S. Evacuation of sick & wounded from forward area proceeded smoothly. 36 "D"s Cars All passed through our A.D.S. Road from VILLERS-PLOUICH to BEAUCAMP much damaged by tanks & Salvage heavy artillery & by shell fire. All hands turned out at dawn to repair & clean road.	CM
	8		Lt THORNHILL M.O.R.C. returned from 2nd Depot bittn. DUISANS. A hired ambulance struck by shell fire at CHARING CROSS Crater. 4 horses of 1st Aid killed & driver severely injured. Much work still necessary on road & A.D.S. to keep Ford Cars running. Services Any. S.B.s no longer required. Lieut THORNHILL detailed for duty at A.D.S.	CM CM
	9			CM
	10		Lieut. THORNHILL sent to 2/1 WARWICKS for duty	CM
	11		A burial party attached to A.D.S. to bury dead in the vicinity of YARA RAVINE. Drawing medical equipment sched. for	CM CM
	12		Lieut. GARRISON M.O.R.C. detailed for duty at & with 2/5 WARWICKS. Evacuation completed for evacuation walking wounded tonight by light railway from TRESCAULT to C.M.D.S. at FINS. Train service of any sort today.	CM

WAR DIARY
or
INTELLIGENCE SUMMARY.
(Erase heading not required.)

Army Form C. 2118.

Place	Date	Hour	Summary of Events and Information	Remarks and references to Appendices
VILLERS	DEC 12		Body of Lt Col BALFOUR 2/7 WORCESTERS Killed in action, conveyed to FINS for burial. Stray Wd pain & all stretcher cases were brought direct to CCS. Arrangements now altered only urgent cases to CCS such cases to be provided with 2d Field Ord. stamped with Fd. Amb. Stamps	Ch1 Ch1
	13		No 9 SB in forward area dismounted its Carbide light	
	14		Transferred from III Corps to V Corps. V Corps Medical Arrangements – fine. Read of over. Sent direct to CCS regarded to be call for ADS & MDS at RUYAULCOURT and Manifield rendered	Ch1 Ch1
	16		New G.S. Wagon + Water Cart received from Ordnance. Lieut PETERSON M.O.R.C. went for to attend a Court Martial at WINCHESTER HUTS and ordered to proceed accordingly. Commenced salving large dump of stretchers from near FARM RAVINE. Dump established in VILLERS-PLOUICH	Ch1 Ch1
	17		War proceeded with at A.D.S. ADS repeatedly shelled heavily. Return brought up by limber at dawn each day. Driver of ration limber wounded when ADS. 312 Ritchie saw by 63rd Div. test took our ADS. on present relief of 61st Dn. by 63rd Capt WOOD to 300R	Ch1 Ch1
	19		Left in forward area till relief complete.	Ch1
	22		Lieut ARNOTT 49 o.R. returned from CCS for duty. Lieuts WILSON & WILLIAMS reported for duty	Ch1 Ch1

WAR DIARY
or
INTELLIGENCE SUMMARY.
(Erase heading not required.)

Army Form C. 2118.

Place	Date	Hour	Summary of Events and Information	Remarks and references to Appendices
VILKEN	DEC 23		Relief of 69th B.W. complete. Capt WOOD returned with men from A.D.S.	Chl
	24		Lieut WILSON M.O.R.C. evacuated to C.C.S. Capt BOLSTER returned for 2/15th A.C.	Chl
	24		Entrained at YTRES for PLATEAU S.E. at 8.0 p.m. on arrival detailed party of men to assist in detraining part of 188 Bde Transport. Marched three to billets in	
BRAY			BRAY-SUR-SOMME arriving about 2.0 a.m Christmas morning.	
	25		Transport proceeded by road with 188 Bde transport left FINS about 7.0 a.m. reached BRAY at 8.0 p.m. Transport travelled empty on account of frozen snow on roads. Equipment carried a lorries apart by train with personnel.	Chl
	25		Opened hospital for Bde sick. Lieut NORTH M.O.R.E. U.S.A. taken as strength a reporting for duty.	Chl Chl
	26		Improving billets weather very cold fuel scarce improving stoves for heating hospital etc.	Chl
	28		The men celebrate Xmas with a dinner. Lieut WILLIAMS detailed for duty with 2/8 WORCESTERS	Chl
	30		Preparing to move to MARCELCAVE. Regents dinner.	Chl
	31		Marched to billets at MARCELCAVE accompanied transport. Hospital opened 34 patients	Chl
MARCELCAVE			26 transferred from BRAY SUR SOMME	

Ch Smith Lt Col RAMC.
O.C. 2/3 S.M.Staffs Amb.

Medical

CONFIDENTIAL

WAR DIARY

OF

2/3RD SOUTH MIDLAND FIELD AMBULANCE.

FROM JANUARY 1ST 1918   TO JANUARY 31ST 1918

(VOLUME   )

MAPS
AMIENS
ST QUENTIN
SHEET 66D

Army Form C. 2118.

WAR DIARY
or
INTELLIGENCE SUMMARY.
(Erase heading not required.)

Instructions regarding War Diaries and Intelligence Summaries are contained in F. S. Regs., Part II. and the Staff Manual respectively. Title pages will be prepared in manuscript.

Place	Date	Hour	Summary of Events and Information	Remarks and references to Appendices
MARCELCAVE Sheet AMIENS G.2.	JAN. 1. 18		Opened hospital for 183 Bde Sick. Capt. W.V. WOOD R.A.M.C. awarded the M.C. in New Years Honours.	App L
	2		Two survivors of 9 men of 183 M.G. Coy. admitted suffering from CO poisoning sustained while sleeping in a billet in the village in which an open brazier was burning coal without adequate ventilation. Inspection by A.D.M.S.	App L
	3			
	4		Route march to WIENCOURT. Roads froze + very slippery.	
	5		Inspection by G.O.C. the Division accompanied by the A.A. + Q.M.G. + the acting Brigadier of 183 Bde.	App L
ROYE (Sheet AMIENS J.4.)	7		Marched with 183 Bde to ROYE. Opened hospital for sick. Motor Ambulance attached to R.F.A. during the move.	App L
GERMAINE Sheet ST QUENTIN B.3.	9		Marched with part of 183 Bde to GERMAINE & FORESTE (Sheet St. QUENTIN 3.6). MATIGNY–DOVILLY Rd Worked with great difficulty with transport. One G.S. Wagon broke down & left behind; Teams of two others too exhausted to proceed beyond DOVILLY. Billeted with 2/2 S.M.Amb. in French Fd. Amb. Lt. ARNOTT left in charge of hospital at ROYE pending removal of sick. Capt. BOLSTER detailed for temporary duty with 2/5 WARWICK BATTN. Lieut. NORTH M.O.R.C. U.S.A. detailed for duty with 2/8 WARWICK Batt.	App L
	10		Main dressing Station + Divl Rest Station opened at point N. of GERMAINE–FORESTE Rd map ref E.17.b.2.8. Sheet 66D. in premises erected by the French for a field ambulance. Premises	App L

Army Form C. 2118.

WAR DIARY
or
INTELLIGENCE SUMMARY.
(Erase heading not required.)

Instructions regarding War Diaries and Intelligence Summaries are contained in F. S. Regs., Part II. and the Staff Manual respectively. Title pages will be prepared in manuscript.

Place	Date	Hour	Summary of Events and Information	Remarks and references to Appendices
GERMAINE E.17.b.28. Sheet 66D	Jan 10		Carried on work hut 100ft by 25ft and a large hangar 110ft x 45ft. Wilt Corkscrew. The French evacuated 4 huts late hangar for our use pending the completion of relief. Military Medals awarded to Sgt. WILKINS, Pte COWLEY and Dr VARNOLD. Dr PATTHIAN to Sgt SEVIER, Dr STEED to Pte JONES. H.S. Transport lines at FORESTE map ref E.16 central sheet 66 D.	CAL CAL
	12		2/2 S.M. Fd. Amb. moved to GERMAINE	
	13		5/3 and 4/3 French Field Ambulance relieved at 4.30 a.m. Officers temp. billets evacuated by French officers at FORESTE. more. Lieut WILLIAMS reported from 2/8 WORCESTERS. Capt. GREEN reported of 2/1st S.M. Ft. Amb. with me the Officer and 100 O.R. arrived & proceeded with billets Lieut A.M. BROOKES proceeded on leave.	CAL
	14		Two Motor Ambulances attached from 31 M.A.C. 146 patients in hospital. Organising hospital in annex. Harken Scabies Isolation Officer Medical Surgical in Beech, Latrins & Cookhouses &c.	CAL CAL 66/12
	15		Personnel of D.S.C. column classified in categories ArB.	
	16		Three motor ambulances attached from 31 M.A.C.	
	17.		Personnel of Detached MT. MT. A.S.C. classified in categories ArB. No 2 Cy A.S.C. at DOUILLY examined & similarly classified.	CAL

WAR DIARY or INTELLIGENCE SUMMARY

Army Form C. 2118.

Place	Date	Hour	Summary of Events and Information	Remarks and references to Appendices
GERMAINE E17b28 Sh51/61D	JAN 18		Capt. BOLSTER reported from 2/5 WARWICKS. No. 1 Coy A.S.C. classified A1B.	Ch
	19		G.O.C. the Division visited the hospital. Lieut NORTH more strict off strength from Jan 17.18. No 2 Coy ASC classified A1B. 3 Officers 240 O.R. DISchain inoculated. ADMS Conference 2.30pm per OSC.	Ch
	20		No 3 Coy A.S.C. classified. Scabies cases transferred for treatment to 2/1 S.M.H. Amb also mumps + measles	Ch
	22		G.O.C. the Div. presented ribbons to officers & men of the R.A.M.C. who had been h immediate awards for gallantry. MAC cars returned & evacuations arranged with O.C. 31 M.A.C. Chief. 5 R men attached for instruction in water duties.	Ch
	23		Emergency medical aid posts established in case of bombing by enemy aeroplanes at DOUILLY and FORESTE. Corps scheme for treatment of cases of gas poisoning distributed in hospital.	Ch
	24		Lieut WILLIAMS MORE detailed to 2/6 GLOUCESTERS vice Capt. BISHOP who was admitted to hospital. SR	Ch
	25		Inspection of hospital by DDMS XVIII Corps. Capt. McCOMBIE RANE reported for duty	Ch Ch

Army Form C. 2118.

WAR DIARY
or
INTELLIGENCE SUMMARY.
(Erase heading not required.)

Instructions regarding War Diaries and Intelligence Summaries are contained in F. S. Regs., Part II and the Staff Manual respectively. Title pages will be prepared in manuscript.

Place	Date	Hour	Summary of Events and Information	Remarks and references to Appendices
GERMAINE E7 b 28 Sheet 11 D	JAN 28		Francherres left vlant by French H.Ambulance sent to HAM by horse transport of the three field ambulances	ChC
			Capt. CLANCY RAMC & Lieut OSSMAN M.O.R.C. USA reported for duty	ChC
	29		Capt. W.E. WALLIS RAMC reported for duty	ChC
	30		Capt. McCOMBIE RAMC detailed for duty with 2/1 Bucks Batt.	ChC
	31		Work of opening & equipping hospital proceeded with. Constructing new cookers. Visit from DDMS Corps. 20 patients in hospital.	

Alander
Lt Col RAMC
OC 2/3 S Midland Ambulance

14 Medical 40/2784 / 9A22

CONFIDENTIAL

WAR DIARY

OF

2/3RD SOUTH MIDLAND FIELD AMBULANCE

FROM 1st FEBRUARY 1918 TO 29th FEBRUARY 1918

(VOLUME   )

COMMITTEE FOR THE
MEDICAL HISTORY OF THE WAR
Date -8 APR 1918

WAR DIARY
INTELLIGENCE SUMMARY.

(Erase heading not required.)

Army Form C. 2118.

Place	Date	Hour	Summary of Events and Information	Remarks and references to Appendices
GERMAINE may nt E7 & 25 Sher 15d	Feb. 2		Capt. WALMSLEY R.A.M.C reported for duty & detailed to D.A.C. at VILLERS ST. CHRISTOPHE.	C/L
	3.		Capt. G.S. CLANCY detailed for duty with 14th Army Fd Art'y Bde.	C/L
			19 class Bmen having completed their training in water duties returned to their units.	C/L
	4.		Capt WALLIS W.E. R.A.M.C to replace Capt. CLANCY with 14 AFA Bde.	W/W
	6.		Capt. WOOD assumed command of Amb. v/ Lt Col. LANDER away on leave.	W/W
	7.		Conference at A.D.M.S. J.O.C.s frostbite-hardness etc & return to medical arrangements in case of retirement.	W/W
	8.		Arrangements for stretcher bearers to conduct sick parade to the Hospital daily for those wanting treatment, also for an inspection of the whole of the two ambulances to weed out those unfit for the necessary amount of walking & carrying required.	W/W
	10.		School of Instruction for Officers Reams. Opened at Ham. Lt OSMAN detailed to attend the course to do work. Capt. CLANCY detailed to Gloucesters.	W/W
	13.		Col. PRYANE D.D.M.S. paid a visit of inspection.	W/W
	14.		Received instructions to collect, check & store medical equipment of the ambulances & field units.	W/W

Army Form C. 2118.

WAR DIARY
or
INTELLIGENCE SUMMARY.
(Erase heading not required.)

Place	Date	Hour	Summary of Events and Information	Remarks and references to Appendices
GERMAINE MAP REF. E7a2.8 Sheet 66D	18.		CAPT WALMESLEY attached to 1/5 GORDON HIGHLANDERS. During the week work of protecting the huts / gun platforms puncture-	
	20.		Visit by DOMS, who laid stress on the arrangements for treating gas cases, particularly in shutting off the respective examinations. Sandbag rooms to make the space of gas transmes entrenchments battery. Stray cats to be now provided for treatment. 17 the eyes with annotates for postentitis &c friendly downwind of the [?] batteries	
	23		Capt WALMESLEY + Lt ARNOT detached to 24 Div 1st ENTRENCHING BATT" on relief of [?] to the unit.	
	25		Lt.Col. C.L. LANDER returned from leave resumed command	
	27		Lt: OSSMAN M.O.R.C. U.S.A. reported for duty from 2/7 WARWICK BATT"	
	28		Col. NIXON R.A.M.C. Consulting Physician of Army visited the Ambulance + inspected Gas Centre	

[signature]
Lt.Col R.A.M.C
O/c 2/3rd S.M. Field Ambulance

26 CONFIDENTIAL

Medical
Vol 23

WAR DIARY

OF

2/3RD SOUTH MIDLAND FIELD AMBULANCE

FROM MARCH 1st 1918 TO MARCH 31st 1918

(VOLUME

COMMITTEE FOR THE
MEDICAL HISTORY OF THE WAR
Date 12 MAY 1918

WAR DIARY or INTELLIGENCE SUMMARY

Army Form C. 2118

MAPS SHEET 66 D AMIENS DIEPPE Part II

Place	Date	Hour	Summary of Events and Information	Remarks and references to Appendices
GERMAINE E.17 a 2.8 Sheet 66D	1916 March 1		Improving Bat Rest Station & Hospital and preparing a Gas Centre in Hangar for treatment of gas cases from 61st & 20th Divs.	Chl
	3		Capt BOLSTER R.A.M.C. rejoined from leave	
			Capt COLEMAN R.A.M.C. reported for duty	Chl
			Capt CLANCY R.A.M.C. posted to 4th S.M. Fd Ambulance	Chl
	7		Lieut L.N. OSSAAN MORE U.S.A. proceeded to a Hospital of the U.S.A. for surgical work.	Chl
	8		Lieut E.V. WHITAKER MORE U.S.A. temporarily attached for duty	Chl
	9		Capt W.V. WOOD R.A.M.C.T. proceeded on leave to England.	
	10		Q.M. & Hon Capt C. MAYES reported for duty from England	
			Capt. I. Van DANDAIGUE R.A.M.C.T.C. reported for duty	Chl
	13		Lieut E.V. WHITAKER MORE U.S.A. detached to 2/1 Ox & Bucks Bn for temporary duty	Chl
			1 Officer & 1 N.C.O.R. attended lectures at BEAUVOIS by Sir H JOHNSTONE	Chl
	15		Capt COLEMAN R.A.M.C. attached 61st Bn 2A Gun Corps as medical officer.	
	15		Conference at H.A.M. of A.Ds. M.S & O.C. Fd Ambulances of XVIII Corps to discuss the question of Fd. Ambulance Equipment and formation of a Corps Receiving Centre.	Chl
	20		Conference of O.C. Fd Ambs. at A.D.M.S Office	Chl

WAR DIARY or INTELLIGENCE SUMMARY

Army Form C. 2118.

Place	Date	Hour	Summary of Events and Information	Remarks and references to Appendices
GERMAINE Map Ref 62c E19 a 2.6	MAR 18		Gas Centre completed with Spray today and letter to hangar & large number of fitters & Hutchitt, & Holdson Corps Apparatus in Rauchstein Ward. Apparatus prepared for inhalation. 4 for aerial training of eyes.	Khaki
	19		Hospital inspected by Maj. General SKINNER D.M.S of Army who inspected inhalation & sprays in tent.	CWL
	20		Acting ADMS 21st Div visited gas centre. Col PRYNNE D.DMS XVIIth Corps visited hospital. Inspected 1 Officer & 16 O.R. admitted, all suffering from gas the result of the premature explosion of our own T.M. gas shells during gas offensive near ST QUENTIN the previous evening. 9 unable & patients in hospital reduced to about 60 by evacuations to the Army Convalescent Depot GAILLY to prepare for reception of alarm of slight gas cases yesterday. All cases fit returned to unit.	CWL CWL CWL
	21		The anticipated German Offensive commenced by an intense bombardment at 4.40 a.m. lasting till 11 a.m. when Crisall to began to arrive back. An abdominal case sent to 41 CCS CUGNY, refused admission so CCS was closed. All cases expected to 45 CCS. HAM. All remaining Sick evacuated from hospital to 61 CCS. Officers Convalescent sent to XVIIth Corps O Rest Sta. at VOYENNES.	

WAR DIARY or INTELLIGENCE SUMMARY.

Army Form C. 2118.

(Erase heading not required.)

Instructions regarding War Diaries and Intelligence Summaries are contained in F.S. Regs., Part II. and the Staff Manual respectively. Title pages will be prepared in manuscript.

Place	Date	Hour	Summary of Events and Information	Remarks and references to Appendices
GERMAINE Sheet 66D F.17.a.8	Mar. 21		During the day 120 Gas cases from 61st & 20th Divns treated at g/s centre evacuated including Capt CLANCY. A deep wounded made attached to evacuated. Total casualties passed through A+D took during the day about 300. 3 Officers + 60 O.R. The rear chiefs concerned about to B/CCS HAM.	CH
	22		Seen an older R+O from ADMS the prepared to move at any moment. All casualties evacuated CHAM.	
MARCHÉ-ALLOUARDE Sheet 66D N.4.C.11.		11 pm	Ordered to move at once to MARCHÉ-ALLOUARDE Sheet 66D. N.4.C.11. All available equipment + hospital stores removed to MT. found temporary dumps at DOUILLY + MATIGNY. Must if had we cleared later in the day to MARCHÉ via NOYENNES. Before hospital be evacuated several German skulls fell in the vicinity. Open hardly were seen to be taking up prepared positions nearby. Casualties passed through A+D took 99 O.R.	CH
	23		C.O. & Capt VAN DAEDALUQUE reconnoitred in direction of HOMBLEUX & found an ADS on NESLE - HAM road at 136.v.1.8. sheet 66D Control established with 12 Bde R.A.P. of Capt MANNEL + Capt COATSWORTH R.A.P. Casualties evacuated by our MT direct to CCS at ROYE. Numbers through A+D took 16. 5 M.A. Cars & 14 M.A. Lorries attached to our HQ at MARCHE. Capt BISHOP in charge at MARCHE Lieut WHITAKER M.O.R.C. U.S.A. reported. About 3:30 p.m. got a verbal order for Staff Officers evacuation of Transport + Ambulance proceeded in direction of ROYE. These ordered to return via the ROYE - NESLE road.	C CH

WAR DIARY or INTELLIGENCE SUMMARY

Army Form C. 2118.

Place	Date	Hour	Summary of Events and Information	Remarks and references to Appendices
MARCHE-ALLOUARDE N&CH 54&D	Mar 24		Work of evacuation pt of casualties proceeded from ADS HOMBLEUX to ROYE. About noon owing to German advance westward from HAM, the ADS was withdrawn across the canal to BREUIL near the church, moving 13 and 7.9 Sh 62 R where post with Spl LEWIS in charge remained at HOMBLEUX. Capt BOLSTER came up with 58 O.R. Capt COATSWORTH R.A.M.C. who had worked at ADS HOMBLEUX the previous day remained attached. A bep mule of casualties dealt with at BREUIL H.T. & remaining personnel moved with ADS etc. for MARCHE to FRANSART Sh 11 66 D 6 & 42. The M.T. & a small party remained at MARCHE under Capt BISHOP. Capts BOLSTER & Van DANDAIGNE with 26 O.R. returned for ADS to FRANSART.	
FRANSART 66 A L Sh 66 (D)	25		The enemy having entered HOMBLEUX the ad post was withdrawn to the canal bank E. of BREUIL + MOYENCOURT, which was manned by Bristol & French troops. A.D.S. withdrawn to CRESSY with base posts at BREUIL to which cars proceeded via MOYENCOURT. Casualties Transp'd A with R 8 officers 156 O.R. 2 Evac with Lt SANFORD at LANEUVOISIN, Lt GALLAGHER at BREUIL + Capt MANUEL at MOYENCOURT. Attached Capt COATSWORTH to & 1 C.O.R. with one car to work with 61st Fd Amb at CRESSI. Moved to BIARRE with Amy personnel + Transport Capt George BISHOP with personnel + M.T. now	CBL

WAR DIARY
or
INTELLIGENCE SUMMARY.

Army Form C. 2118.

Place	Date	Hour	Summary of Events and Information	Remarks and references to Appendices
FRANSART G.24.a.2 13.H.Q.	Mar. 25		Adv. from MARCHÉ ALLOUARDE to BIARRE. O.C. Adv. proceeded to Convoy via BALATRE & GRUNY to FRESNOY-LES-ROYE. Adv. was met by Capt BOLSTER from FRANSART that his disposal was to the enemy to near VILLERS	
WARVILLERS Q27aMAIN 13.H.Q.			Several men picked up at FRANSART who could not be accounted for, spent the night under transport. Wood parties. O.C. and Capt BISHOP reported at WARVILLERS. Cpl Little J Waugh & H Stock & Officers 30 O.R. Cpt WOOD returned from leave.	C.H.
	26		Cpt COATSWORTH returned to Div HQ. He detached Car 278 OC reported, but except Pte CLARK was the only 2 cars moved to proceed forthwith to MARCELCAVE. WARVILLERS to FRESNOY-EN-CHAUSSÉE 2 men could proceed forthwith	
MORISEL (Sect. AMER) @Feb 60 HAILLES Q.9.b.5	27		MORISEL. Evacuated whole west of the village. Lt WHITAKER detached (8 clerks with 2/2 S.M.Fd Amb at MORISEL. C.H. Stretcher bearers Order not to man to HAILLES; available tentage in village with 61st BRITransport. Couldn't find Ambulance. 2 officers. 172 O.R.	C.H.
	28		A.D.S. found at VILLERS BRETONNEUX by Capt WOOD & BISHOP. 3 cars attached to several convoys.	
		4.30pm	Found Div first in hands of MARCELCAVE. Cavalry Escort and took 4 officers & JBR. Cars seeing to man our Amb. from VILLERS-BRETONNEUX on the road to East end of CACHY despatch riders brought verbal order from MOJAS to return to GENTELLES when in Adv. was at once	
GENTELLES R.19.H.1 13.H.Q			turned back large number of casualties who were the enemy. Capt WOOD conducted transport via BOVES	C.H.
			was pursued.	

WAR DIARY or INTELLIGENCE SUMMARY

Army Form C. 2118.

Place	Date	Hour	Summary of Events and Information	Remarks and references to Appendices
GENTELLES (Annex) @ F52	April 29		Bearer post formed at VILLERS BRETONNEUX by Contact established with the RAPs. R.O. Cathy with MARCELCAVE & a BOIS DE HANGAR. Casualties evacuated by one car from VILLERS BRETONNEUX to ACS. Others by MAC cars & lorries to CCS at NAMPS. A hvy shock casualties attached to 9th Hrs + 45? OR thryt and lost. 13 donkeys imported for use with bat.	Ok
	30		Bearer post at VILLERS-BRETONNEUX Sta withdrawn to a point a CACHY Rd owing to tear RAPs withdrawn to the Station + LONE TREE. A party Bearers sent to MOR at LONE TREE S. Rly pst formed. Bearer post established at CACHY. Casualties thryt and Evack nec	Ok
	31		18th Div relieved 61st pstn at CACHY. VILLERS hardened. HGS at GENTELLES retained as Rlf Bl.on remained there in support. Part of ADS destroyed by shell in camellia & two in walls. Two MOs 17 OR. with the cars at ADS (Remainder) had moved to LILLE in BOVES with transport. Casualties thryt acetone 30	Ok
BOVES April 1 @ E54				Ok

Alexander Lt Col RAMC

MEDICAL Ya 24

140/2900

A CONFIDENTIAL

WAR DIARY.

OF

2/3rd. SOUTH MIDLAND FIELD AMBULANCE

FROM April 1st 1918   TO April 31st 1918.

(VOLUME   )

COMMITTEE FOR THE
MEDICAL HISTORY OF THE WAR
Date -6 JUN 1918

Army Form C. 2118.

DIEPPE 16. HAZEBROUCK 5ᴬ
AMIENS 14. SHEET 36ᴬ

WAR DIARY
or
INTELLIGENCE SUMMARY.
(Erase heading not required.)

Instructions regarding War Diaries and Intelligence Summaries are contained in F. S. Regs., Part II. and the Staff Manual respectively. Title pages will be prepared in manuscript.

Place	Date	Hour	Summary of Events and Information	Remarks and references to Appendices
BOVES (AMIENS 14) @ E 5.2.	April 1		ADS at GENTELLES Capt WOOD in charge. Few casualties. Divisional relief pending.	CM
	2		Two cars detached for duty with DAC & Field Artillery during the mov	CM
	3		On car sent on with 189 Bde to billet in HEUCOURT area shell (DIEPPE 16) OK 6.2. Relief complete about 4.0 am. 189 Bde troops followed, Ambulance cars to embussing point N of BOVES. Capt WOOD evacuated more than 60 casualties from GENTELLES before handing over to FAMB 9/15ᵗʰ Div	CM
PICQUIGNY (AMIENS 14) (B 4.6.	4		March complete to PICQUIGNY (B 7.3) (Met AMIENS 7) where we billetted for the night The Ambulance observed march & arrived at ST MAULVIS (Sheet DIEPPE 1) K 4.6. Opened hospital.	CM
ST MAULVIS (DIEPPE 1) K 4.6.	5		Kit inspection of entire unit M.O's attend daily 4/5 GORDONS & N.8 B.Coy A.S.C.	CM
	6		Inclusively equipment &c	CM
	7		Issues of form & Odd Rear Details.	CM
	9		Instructions received to prepare for subsequent Waggons cleaned & packed. Received bottles & provided with clean cloths.	CM
	10		Lt GRAN RAMC. attached for duty to 4/5 GORDON HIGHLAND Bn. Hospital evacuated except 13 pts who have turned.	CM

Army Form C. 2118.

WAR DIARY
or
INTELLIGENCE SUMMARY.
(Erase heading not required.)

Instructions regarding War Diaries and Intelligence Summaries are contained in F.S. Regs., Part II. and the Staff Manual respectively. Title pages will be prepared in manuscript.

Place	Date	Hour	Summary of Events and Information	Remarks and references to Appendices
ST MAULVIS (DIEPPE 16) (2)K.18	April 10		Moved off in the evening transport in advance to entrain at HANGEST-SUR-SOMME. Shell AMIENS to L.Krais at 1130 a.m. on the 11th. Capt BISHOP sent on with 183 Bde billetting party.	D.a.s.t. C/cl
	11		Arrived HANGEST at 10 a.m. men provided with hot tea. Train to horse lett. Entrainment party arrived from our H.T. CAPT VAN DANDAIGUE medical attached to the entrainment. Capt BOLSTER sent on to detrainment at CALONNE SUR LA LYS. Destination changed to STEENBECQUE (D.F.18.) Shell HAZEBROUCK 6A. Journey delayed owing to many trains trailing into BETHUNE by enemy shell fire. Arrived at 3 p.m.	C/cl
ST.VENANT Sh.E.36.a P.q.b.			Made to ST.VENANT billetted for the night at the Portugese hospital ASILE D'ALIENES (sheet 36a P.q.b.) Distributed to various quarters from 183 Bde. a short distance from CALONNE STEENBECQUE.	C/cl
	12	10.40 a	2/Lt 7th and arrived at 5 a.m. on 12th from M.D.T. Hospital heavily shelled. Staff Sgt ROACH & actg S/Sgt SEVIER, Cpl BOORMAN & 18 Privates wounded. Ptes COWLES M.M., MILSON, HARRIS, FORD, GRIEVE & GROVE killed, five of these were killed whilst attending to a wounded Officer.	
GUARBECQUE O.II.C.5.6 Sheet 36a			Capt. WOOD moved H.T. & supply personnel to O.II.C.5.8 (Sheet 36a) near village of GUARBECQUE and so killed there (a temporary hospital reception) formed. Capt BISHOP remained at the HOSPITAL ST.VENANT until the wounded were evacuated. When he handed over to the 2/1 Field Amb. and rejoined HQ. C.O. with C Section Bearers went forward to ST FLORIS and formed an A.D.S. at P.6.7.5.8. Stretchers H.C. W. W. W. cooled with RAP. of 183 Bde. to which bearer Squads were attached. Casualties cleared for ST FLORIS by cars. Considerable number evacuated. Late in the day ADS retired.	

Army Form C. 2118.

WAR DIARY
or
INTELLIGENCE SUMMARY.
(Erase heading not required.)

Place	Date	Hour	Summary of Events and Information	Remarks and references to Appendices
GUARBECQUE O31.c.5.8 Sheet 36a	Ap. 12		to P.3.C.05 (Sheet 36) on account of enemy advance. Officers and P. & NCOs where transferred for the night. Capt WILKINS left in charge.	CdL
	13		Rear Hd Qrs established at P.3.C.44. Officers and men went up by 5 VEHANT.	CdL
	14		Advanced echelon H.Q. by M.A.C. Cars by 8.30 a.m. A.D.S. established at P.S.C.O.9 on Canal bank. Capt BOLSTER in charge. Capt BISHOP & A/D.S.	
			Capt SCOTT-WILLIAMSON rejoined the Division having been liberated from GERMANS, 2 months prisoner, and temporarily attached to this unit. 18 Reinforcements taken on strength.	
			Capt S.R.GIBBD reported for duty & posted to 2/5 GLOUCESTER Bn.	CdL
	15		D.R.S. special camouflage work at AIRE (N28d25) with one tent sub-division & equipment. Capt SCOTT-WILLIAMSON in charge.	CdL
			Capt BOLSTER went to ENGLAND on expiration of his contract.	CdL
	16		Capt W.V. WOOD in charge of A.D.S.	CdL
	17		Capt BISHOP in charge of A.D.S. D.R.S. receive 100 patients & treat Scabies.	CdL
	18		Capt VAN DARDAIGNE in charge of A.D.S.	CdL
	19		A.D.S. moved to P.3.C.44. will leave patients at P.S.C.09. H.Q. heavily shelled for 24 hours by c.12" gun. No casualties.	CdL
LAMBRES Sheet 36a	20		Lt BUGGE & MORE U.S.A. reported for duty. Owing to continued hostile shelling near H.Q. the H.Q. & Transport moved back to billets at LAMBRES N10d Sheet 36a. 20 Reinforcements received & taken on strength.	CdL

Army Form C. 2118.

WAR DIARY
or
INTELLIGENCE SUMMARY.
(Erase heading not required.)

Instructions regarding War Diaries and Intelligence Summaries are contained in F.S. Regs., Part II and the Staff Manual respectively. Title pages will be prepared in manuscript.

Place	Date	Hour	Summary of Events and Information	Remarks and references to Appendices
LAMOTRES N.10.U.C.4. Sheet 36A	21		Dul Rev Ste al AIRE further developed, receiving up to 150 patients	Old
	22		Capt BISHOP R.A.M.C. returns to ENGLAND on expiration of his contract.	Old
	23		Sgt BROWN appointed Acting Staff Sergeant of B Section.	Old
			Work at A.D.S. + D.R.S. continued. Evacuation of sick wounded proceeding smoothly	Old
	24		Capt VANDAIGUE R.A.M.C. T.C. evacuated to C.C.S. sick	
			Capt WICKERT M.O.R.C. via returned from ARGYLE + SUTHERLAND HIGHLAND Bn by	
			LT A.S. BUGBE M.O.R.C.	
			Capt H.F. WICKERT M.O.R.C. taken on strength evacuated sick to C.C.S.	Old
			Capt DALE-WOOD R.A.M.C. + Capt T.L. BUTLER R.A.M.C. reported for duty	Old
			Capt S.R. GLEED H.R.A.M.C. struck off strength on personal appointment 2/5 GLOUCESTER R.	Old
	25		Sgt O. Bates LEWIS L/Cpl S. REDDING Pte F.G. VINCENT, S.E. MACHIN, W.H. PAYNE awarded the	
			Military Medal. A.D.S. visited by D.D.M.S. Corps.	
	26		LT G.K. STONE R.A.M.C. S.R. taken on strength. Sqd of A.D.S. completed	Old
	27		Commenced salvaging material also returned to first old C.C.S. site near HAZEBROUCK.	Old
	28		Salvage continued. D.R.S. inspected by D.D.M.S. XI Corps.	Old
	29		Capt G. SCOTT-WILLIAMSON R.A.M.C. posted to 2/1 S.M. Fd. Amb. Capt A. RADFORD R.A.M.C. and	Old

Army Form C. 2118.

WAR DIARY
or
INTELLIGENCE SUMMARY.

(Erase heading not required.)

Instructions regarding War Diaries and Intelligence Summaries are contained in F. S. Regs., Part II. and the Staff Manual respectively. Title pages will be prepared in manuscript.

Place	Date	Hour	Summary of Events and Information	Remarks and references to Appendices
HINGES (April 06) Sheet 36. April	29		Capt J.E.J. ROCHE-KELLY RAMC T.C. taken on the strength of the unit. Capt T.L. BUTLER transferred to 307 Bde R.F.A. vice Capt A. SANDFORD.	
	30		Threed disinfector salved from forward area N.E. of ST VENANT. Work at A.T.S. & D.R.S. continued also salvage for A.C.C.S. site.	Ctd

Clarke Lt. Cl. RAMC
Oc 93rd 1st Field Ambulance

MEDICAL Vol 25

140/283.

CONFIDENTIAL
WAR DIARY
OF

2/3rd South Midland Field Ambulance

From 1st May 1918 To 31st May 1918

(VOLUME   )

COMMITTEE FOR THE
MEDICAL HISTORY OF THE WAR
Date 9 JUL 1918

WAR DIARY or INTELLIGENCE SUMMARY

Army Form C. 2118.

MAPS. Sheet 36A

Place	Date	Hour	Summary of Events and Information	Remarks and references to Appendices
LAMBRES N1 of 61. Sheet 36A	May 2		Bomb dropped by E.A. near B section billet at 4.0 p.m. S.Sgt BROWN & Pte STEVENS slightly wounded	CWL
	3		Work of improving ADS and DRS continued	CWL
	4		Capt. DALE WOOD RAMC detailed for duty at CRS. Inder May WATERHOUSE P/2/2 Fit And	CWL
			Capt. W.V. WOOD gazetted to the rank of acting Major	CWL
	7		Capt DALE WOOD reported back for duty on closing of CRS at RELY	CWL
			Capt ROCHE-KELLEY RAMC and Lt STONE RAMC Sr. detailed for duty at DRS and	CWL
			ADS to relieve said the way for change	CWL
	10		Driver F.J. JENKINS MT ASC attached 2/3 Fd Amb awarded the Military Medal	CWL
	13		D.A.S. P.Army Inspected DRS	CWL
	14		ADS severely shelled in the afternoon Capt DALE WOOD in charge No casualties to personnel	CWL
			One motor car damaged and an hire slightly wounded ADS removed to Pt C 61 Sheet 36A	CWL
	15		Patients at DRS evacuated to XI C.R.S. — DRS to be used for treatment	CWL
			Minimal Scabies, local sick and as a station for treatment of slightly gassed cases	CWL
	17		Bomb night of the 16-17 AIRE heavily bombed by EA much damage done BRS untouched	CWL
			A few military & civilian casualties to dealt with at LAMBRES Casualties to C.C.S.	CWL
	18		Enemy Aged Post formed at LAMBRES	CWL

Army Form C. 2118.

WAR DIARY
or
INTELLIGENCE SUMMARY.
(Erase heading not required.)

Instructions regarding War Diaries and Intelligence Summaries are contained in F. S. Regs., Part II and the Staff Manual respectively. Title pages will be prepared in manuscript.

Place	Date	Hour	Summary of Events and Information	Remarks and references to Appendices
LANGRES N.O. 161 Sheet 3. A	18		Capt. DALE WOOD detached to Xt Corps School vice Capt TOBIAS Rtns. at his later. a the thought of the wind.	CUC
	20		The men wrangled by local pop E.A. in A.R.E. Work positively almost precluding W.A.O.T. and Canal bank Post	OKc
	22		Capt. RIDFORD Rtn. et. attached to Military Cars	Clli
	24		Rrtn. work continued	Clli
	25		A.D.M.S. and the DAHPAM G. inspect the N.B. of the Ambulance.	Ckc
	26		C.O. met the 9 North Mid. Field Amb. 115 Suffolks + 1st Lancs. at AIRE Station on their arrival to far the 163 Bde to replace the three Scottish Bns.	Clli
	27		Arranged sick collection from new By	Clli
	28		Lt. STONE sent to No. 1 C.C.S. for Temporary duty. Capt. TOBIAS Rtn. to DRS	Clli
	29		Bdys the lines on ordered of RAMC of the Division approved as suggested by ADMS. It carries to 18" square of dull clay colour on which is divided up a blue surmounted by the nuf of the F.A.	Clli
			The square being let oblique	
	30		Methied Board arranged for telegraphing dis/Corps at 9.0 p.	Clli

Orlando W. O. PMot
Of 2/2nd. S. M. Field Ambulance.

MEDICAL

16 WR 26
June 1918. 40/30%.

CONFIDENTIAL
WAR DIARY
OF
2/3RD SOUTH MIDLAND FIELD AMBULANCE

FROM 1ST JUNE 1918 TO 30TH JUNE 1918

(VOLUME   )

COMMITTEE FOR THE
MEDICAL HISTORY OF THE WAR
Date 7 AUG 1918

MAPS. 36A (SHEET)

Army Form C. 2118.

WAR DIARY
or
INTELLIGENCE SUMMARY.
(Erase heading not required.)

Instructions regarding War Diaries and Intelligence Summaries are contained in F. S. Regs, Part II. and the Staff Manual respectively. Title pages will be prepared in manuscript.

Place	Date	Hour	Summary of Events and Information	Remarks and references to Appendices
LAMBRES N10b 6.0 Sheet 36a	June 1		Capt ROCHE-KELLY detailed with one motor ambulance to accompany the transport of the three Scotch Battalion leaving the division to ARRAS on a two days march.	CLR
	2		Official postcard for registration of parliamentary voters of the B.E.F issued to personnel.	CLR
	3		Company camp at LAMBRES	CLR
	5		Dugout at n. shed at canal point P.52.2.0 sheet 36a, completed capable of accom dely 9 totale can n trif three.	CLR
	6		Under instructions from ADMS carpenters erected sanitary appliances, tops of latrines & urinals to fn. ho. of divisional units. Continued dry weather.	CLR
	7			CLR
	9		Capt TOBIAS RAMC sr. detailed for duty with 2/4 Oxfordshire & Buckinghamshire Light Infantry (Battalion, relieving Capt SHIELDS RAMC Sch.	CLR
	10		During the time the Ambulance be. been at LAMBRES route march, three weekly & physical drill daily have been carried out, also lectures to Nurses, Orderlies & general duty men on surg+ physiology & sanitation by the officers Capt RADFORD RAMC deputes to attend to No 68 Labour (from Battalion) during absence of their M.O.s	CLR

WAR DIARY or INTELLIGENCE SUMMARY

Army Form C. 2118.

Place	Date	Hour	Summary of Events and Information	Remarks and references to Appendices
LAMBRES N.16.6.0. Sheet 36.ª	JUNE 12		During this month a large number of cases of a short febrile disease similar to influenza occurred in the division. The chief symptoms were sudden onset, high pyrexia, sore throat, myalgic pains, headache, pain at back of the eye. Some mild bronchitis usually present. Tongue coated. Duration usually 3 or 4 days. Convalescence usually rapid without sequelae. Pathologists report presence of B. pneumo. bacillus in throat swabs.	CW.
	13		Personnel of the F.A. does not appear to have had from a third to no half of their strength affected.	CW CW
	15		Continued dry weather, roads very dusty. Work of improving dugout accommodation at the A.D.S. relay post continued.	CW
BERGUETTE O.16.C.6.6.	17		Marched from LAMBRES to BERGUETTE taking over the M.D.S. from the 2/1 Field Ambulance. Also the A.D.S. at GUARBECQUE and the forward posts of right Sector of Divisional front.	CW
	19		The A.D.S. of left Sector at P.2.a.6.1. handed over to 2/2 F.A. withdrawn post of tpl sect Camp SHIELDS Camp attached to tpg from duty. Advanced Car Post established at P.24.6.3.3 and P.17.a.0.2. to which cars run on horse.	CW CW
	20		Telephoned for far the N. sluff Bn. Hd. at CARVIN FARM and LES AMUSOIRES respectively. Cars with drivers kept at PARÉ on SIEVENANT - BUSNES Rd. Two cars kept at farm on BUSNES - ROBECQ Rd at P.24.6.60. Repair of roads in area ROBECQ proceeded with & fresh late personnel F.A.	CW CW

WAR DIARY
INTELLIGENCE SUMMARY.
(Erase heading not required.)

Army Form C. 2118.

Place	Date	Hour	Summary of Events and Information	Remarks and references to Appendices
BERGUETTE O1bc66 Sheet 36A	JUNE 21		Capt RADFORD R.A.M.C. Capt ROCHE-KELLY sick. Capt ROCHE-KELLY takes over Labour Group.	Chl Ch
	22		Hospital accommodation increased by transferring Portuguese Tent from GUARBECQUE to BERGUETTE. Arrivals at ADS + attached Labour Group via Capt ROCHE-KELLY	
	23		Capt JEPSON R.A.M.C. from 61st M.G. Bn. arrivals at ADS sick. Lieut STONE reports for duty from 1st Army School and detailed for duty at ADS with care of the sick of 2/6 Warwicks in billets at GUARBECQUE. Lieut BLAKELEY Capt C. of 10th Canadian Field Ambulance reports for temporary duty. Placed i/charge of Labour Group. Court of Enquiry assembled to report on the absence without leave of Pte SCOTT No. 252366 who went to ENGLAND on leave on 6/3/18 did not return. Was found by the police & in minors. Procedures. Major W.V.WOBB RAMC. Member Capt SHIELDS RAMC & Capt JEPSON.	18th Ambulance did not sit Chl Chl
	24		Infantry Hospital Nevention now opened	
	25		Camp opened by 2/2 F.A.M. at TREZENNES for reception of cases of influenza. Skin deport at AIRE closed. Pts transferred to 2/2nd Fd Amb at MOLINGHEM	Chl
	26		Lt BLAKELEY C.A.M.C. rejoins his unit. Capt RADFORD resumes charge of Labour Group. Capt ROCHE-KELLY RAMC leave to report to War Office on expiration of contract. Capt TOBIAS RAMC SR reports for duty	Chl

Army Form C. 2118.

WAR DIARY
or
INTELLIGENCE SUMMARY.
(Erase heading not required.)

Instructions regarding War Diaries and Intelligence Summaries are contained in F. S. Regs., Part II. and the Staff Manual respectively. Title pages will be prepared in manuscript.

Place	Date	Hour	Summary of Events and Information	Remarks and references to Appendices
BERGUETTE 01bc 66 Sheet 3A	JUNE 26		Assisted in transporting repatriated sick to camp at TREIZENNES.	CM Cht
	27		Improving Camp. Attended interview with Pres. meeting with parcel around hospital tent.	
	29		Submitted scheme for retaining prisoners at AIRE formerly used as DRS as a provisional go centre to ADMS. Camp inspected at BERGUETTE inspected by G.O.C. Major-General DUNCAN accompanied by AA+QMG and ADMS.	CM Cht
	30		Continued fine and dry weather.	

[signature]
Lt. Col. PARK
O/C 23rd S.M. Field Ambulance

MEDICAL 90/27

CONFIDENTIAL

WAR DIARY

OF

2/3RD. SOUTH MIDLAND FIELD AMBULANCE

FROM 1st JULY 1918 TO 31st JULY 1918

(VOLUME)

Army Form C. 2118.

MAPS SHEETS 36A and 27

WAR DIARY
or
INTELLIGENCE SUMMARY.

(Erase heading not required.)

Instructions regarding War Diaries and Intelligence Summaries are contained in F. S. Regs., Part II. and the Staff Manual respectively. Title pages will be prepared in manuscript.

Place	Date	Hour	Summary of Events and Information	Remarks and references to Appendices
BERGUETTE O16.c.6.6. Sheet 36a	JULY 1		Capt. A. RADFORD R.A.M.C.T. promoted to the rank of Acting Major whilst commanding a Section of the Field Ambulance to date from April 19	Chl
	2		Medical Arrangements of V Army received under those administration the XI Corps came yesterday, arrangements practically identical with those of 1st Army previously in force	Chl
	3		1st Lieut T.A. McSWEENY M.O.R.C. and Lieut P. THOMPSON M.O.R.C. reported for duty	Chl
	4		Conference at DDMS office to discuss the medical arrangements of 9th Div' during their recent attack.	Chl
	5		Preparing road at BERGUETTE to facilitate passage of cars to evacuate wounds	Chl
	6		Continued fine dry weather	Chl
	7		1st Lieut S.H. WOOD M.O.R.C. U.S.A. posted for duty	Chl
	8		Orders read of relief of division by 74 Divs on the 10-12 inst. Acting ADMS 74 Div visited ambulances with a view to taking over. Thunderstorm with refreshing rain after long drought.	Chl Chl
	9		Capt TOBIAS detailed for duty with RE's during absence of Capt. RENNIE on leave. Details of impending relief arranged with O.C. 230 Field Ambulance	Chl
	10		Major DOUBBLE with detachment of 230 "F.A. arrived and went over forward area of our sector. Maj WOOD with B Section marched to billets at BOURECQ V.I.C. Sheet 36A Head Ambulance detailed to follow. Bar of 183 pole on the march on the night of 10-11-	Chl

Army Form C. 2118

WAR DIARY
or
INTELLIGENCE SUMMARY.
(Erase heading not required.)

Instructions regarding War Diaries and Intelligence Summaries are contained in F. S. Regs., Part II. and the Staff Manual respectively. Title pages will be prepared in manuscript.

Place	Date	Hour	Summary of Events and Information	Remarks and references to Appendices
BERGUETTE O.K.C. 66	July 11		Remainder of Unit with exception of Major RADFORD and 7 O.R. marched to BOURECQ. HQ established at V.I.C.3.6. Test Hospital opened for Brigade sick. A Section bivouac in field near hospital. B.&C. and Transport in billets. Rain.	C.H.L.
BOURECQ V.I.C.3.6. Sheet 36c	12		Lt. STONE R.A.M.C. detailed for Temporary duty with 2/4 R. BERKS Bn.	C.H.L.
	13		Improving & cleaning up camp & billets - erecting sheds, &c. Major RADFORD R.A.M.C. goes on leave to DEAUVILLE. Routine training proceeded with.	C.H.L.
	14		Conference of Fd. Ambulance Commanders at ADMS Office on training scheme whilst in rest. Showery weather. Orders rec'd from G.S. 61st Divn through ADMS (Lelong) that the Divn. less 183 Inf Bde is in G.H.Q Reserve at 24 hr notice and that 183 Inf Bde is in G.H.Q Reserve at 8 hour notice.	C.H.L.
	15		O.C.s Parade & Kit Inspections held.	C.H.L.
	16		Instructional classes for Officers & men of the unit commenced. Conference at DDMS Office XI Corps.	C.H.L.
	17		Heavy thunderstorm during early morning. Training continued.	C.H.L.
	18		Orders rec'd for ADMS to reconnoitre right flank of XI Corps front. Warning order rec'd to move N.of AIRE with 184 Inf Bde Group.	C.H.L.
RINCQ H.19.d.9.9. Sheet 36c	19		Marched with 184 Inf Bde to area N.W. of AIRE. Ambulance bivouac in field at RINCQ H.19.d.9.9.	C.H.L.
	20		Hospital opened (tent) for sick &c. of 184 Bde Group. 184 Bde Band play to unit in the evening. Thunder storms & heavy rain.	C.H.L.
	21		Advised by ADMS that 61 Divn is at 8 hours notice as G.H.Q. reserve. Warning order rec'd to move on 22nd. Hospital & personnel moved to adjoining field. Reconnoitre left flank of XI Corps front with reference to Divl defence scheme.	C.H.L.

WAR DIARY
or
INTELLIGENCE SUMMARY.
(Erase heading not required.)

Army Form C.

Place	Date	Hour	Summary of Events and Information	Remarks and references to Appendices
RINCQ H|q d qq Sheet 21 c 2	July 22		Order recd for 183 Fd Amb to move to HEURINGHEM Area A14. Sheet 26". Marched at 10 p.m. from RINCQ via REBECQ, Scatties Depot with patients from Fd. Ambulance.	C/c/L
QUIESTEDE A28.b.1.3.	23		Reopening hospital. Provisional defence situation recd. and order for ADMS & reconnoitre & report on scheme of evacuation from 183 & Bde front extending from CHERTRE-FLETRE to R.31.c.88. Sheet 27. Conference of O.C. Fd. Ambulance at ADMS Office in re enemy to discuss scheme. D.D.M.S XV Corps visited Dvl Rear S.C. 61 Div in XV Corps. II Army 29 Div	C/c/L
	24		Capt RADFORD returned from leave. Col. MOOR D.D.M.S XV Corps visited the camp and hospl plans for establishment of a Corps for treatment of Spin Affections in field adjoining the camp.	C/c/L C/c/L C/c/L C/c/L
	25		Routine duties. Much rain. Fine weather.	
	26		Major General DUNCAN G.O.C 61 Div visited D.R.S.	
	27		XI Corps Sports at ROQUETOIRE. Ambulance wagon and water cart unserviceable sent 2. Water cart left connection DDMS XI Corps. Very wet.	C/c/L
	28		C.O. with ADMS reconnoitre forward area of XV Corps left sector. Proceeding with XV Corps Spec. Centre erection of half tents.	C/c/L
	29		Reconnaissance of forward area of Majors RADFORD & Lt THOMPSON. Warning notice recd of move into XI Corps area	C/c/L
	30		Field Ambulance Sports held. Attended by DDMS XV Corps ADMS distributed prizes. Very fine day. Sports organised by Major WOOD & Lt Major PELLY very successful.	C/M

Army Form C.

WAR DIARY
or
INTELLIGENCE SUMMARY.

(Erase heading not required.)

Instructions regarding War Diaries and Intelligence Summaries are contained in F.S. Regs., Part II. and the Staff Manual respectively. Title pages will be prepared in manuscript.

Place	Date	Hour	Summary of Events and Information	Remarks and references to Appendices
QUESTEDE A 28 b. 13 Sheet 28A	July 30		Order recd to march with 183 If Bde to #1 FONTES tomorrow. sent to Lt Col R. to give him & piece and with construction of Skin Centre.	Ch.l
"	31		Major RADFORD RAMC sent on to billet Fd Amb at FONTES with MRC and Tent Subdivision of C Section to Opu Hospital at FONTES. Remainder of Unit marched with 183 Inf Bde leaving at 10.30 p.m. after handing over Tent retend etc to 135 Field Ambulance	Ch.l

Alexander
Lt. Col RAMC
O/c 23rd. S.M. Field Ambulance.

MEDICAL

9 August 1918

CONFIDENTIAL

WAR DIARY

Vol 28
40/3200.

OF

2/3RD. SOUTH MIDLAND FIELD AMBULANCE

From 1st August 1918 To 31st August 1918

(VOLUME   )

WAR DIARY or INTELLIGENCE SUMMARY

Army Form C. 2118.

MAP SHEET 36A

Place	Date	Hour	Summary of Events and Information	Remarks and references to Appendices
FONTES N29 + 30 Sheet 36c	Aug 1		Arrived at FONTES at 4.0 a.m. Opened hospital for Bde Sick. 40 patients transported from QUIESTEDE to FONTES. Fine weather.	C/M
	2		Div. Rest Sn. closed & transferring patients to XICCS 2/3 Field Ambulance. Much rain.	C/M C/M
	3		Returned to Ordnance and Adm Depot N.S. the greater part of B Section Mobilization Equipment 14 Fd Ambulance at BOESEGHEM relief by Cycles from Aug 6.18	C/M
	4		Warning order not of impending move to relieve 5 Div. followed by Corps Order No. 65 to relieve 14 Fd Ambulance at BOESEGHEM. MRC detached for temporary duty with 2/2 Fd Amb. Two lorry cars lent by Lce McSWEENEY & WOOD.	
			The following promotions notified from Central Corps Orders received today. Sgt HOBBS promoted to rank of Staff Sgt. Sgt. (Act. Sgt. Maj.) PELLEY " Staff Sgt. Cpl. (Act Sgt) BURGESS " Sergeant Pte (Act Cpl) SLADE " Corporal Pte SWIFT " Corporal Pte DIXON " Corporal	C/M
	5		A Section Transport and 12 O.R. sent forward to BOESEGHEM as an advanced party to commence relief of 14 Fd Ambulance.	C/M
BOESEGHEM T9 + 8c Sheet 36c	6		Ambulance moved with about 20 patients to BOESEGHEM and took over from 14 Field Ambulance hospital accommodation, gas cases & scabies. Personnel conveyed in fine lorries. Recommitted forward area.	C/M

Army Form C. 2118.

WAR DIARY
or
INTELLIGENCE SUMMARY.
(Erase heading not required.)

Instructions regarding War Diaries and Intelligence Summaries are contained in F.S. Regs., Part II and the Staff Manual respectively. Title pages will be prepared in manuscript.

Place	Date	Hour	Summary of Events and Information	Remarks and references to Appendices
BOESEGHEM I 9 a 8.3 Sheet 3.69	Aug 7		Attended Conference at 7.45 pm at ADMS office. Rcd instructions to open an ADS. at HAVERSKERQUE. MERVILLE Rd. Detailed Major RADFORD to take S.B., E LANCS B + 1st SUFFOLKS, proceeded with party of NCO's + 1 wounded for an ADS. ADS established at 10.30 p.m. at J 28 d 4.8 Major Radford in charge. Major West detailed for duty in place of O.C. 57 Sanitary Section BOESEGHEM S/s LEWIS + 5 men detailed for duty against mosquitos in the front of NIEPPE in continuance of 5th Divl Scheme.	
	8		Car loading post established at J.30.d.5.1 in advance of ADS. Specially Sqn placed in le SART.	Ch.L
	9		DMS 1st Army Major Gen. GERRARD visited the Ambulance H.Q. + Section Hospital	Ch.L
	10		Advanced base post established at K.25 d.15. Orders received from ADMS to cooperate with 2/2 Fd Amb in preparation for attack on Leffrinck's Point at dawn on the 11th.	Ch.L
	11		Six bearer squads attached to 2/2 to assist in evacuation. Six horsed Ambulance two from each Fd Amb report to CO in forward area to assist evacn, walking wounded if necessary. Casualties normally few in attack. Extracting exceeded by Lightrailway. Other transport not required. Number of casualties small.	Ch.L
	12		Routine work, improving hospital accommodation. Continued fine weather	Ch.L
	13		Mosquito Cte in the Forest rehearsed. ADS. equipped with latest exchange of clothing for general patrol.	Ch.L

Army Form C. 2118.

WAR DIARY
or
INTELLIGENCE SUMMARY.
(Erase heading not required.)

Instructions regarding War Diaries and Intelligence Summaries are contained in F. S. Regs., Part II. and the Staff Manual respectively. Title pages will be prepared in manuscript.

Place	Date	Hour	Summary of Events and Information	Remarks and references to Appendices
BOESEGHEM 17d 83 Sheet 9k e	Aug 14		Rec'd order for A.D.S. to establish a centre for reception & disposal of all ground cases from the division. Major WOOD appointed i/c charge of 9p. Cases	Chl.
	15		Col. WRIGHT D.D.M.S. X"Corps inspected the Hospital. Major General DUNCAN G.O.C. 61 Div visited the Hospital	Chl
	16		Major RADFORD R.A.M.C. detached for temporary duty with 2/2 Fd Amb. in charge of EDITH A.D.S. Capt TOBIAS in charge of FORGE A.D.S. Lieut EDMONDS R.A.M.C. U.S.A. reported for duty from 2/2 Fd Amb.	Chl Chl
	17		Five Small Nissen Huts erected to extra accommodation for ground patients. To be erected by R.E.'s	Chl Chl
	18		Major RADFORD R.A.M.C. returned from duty with 2/2 Fd Amb. Lt. EDMONDS R.A.M.C. ret back to 2/2 Fd Amb.	Chl
	19		Excavation for Nissen Huts commenced. Continued fine weather	Chl
	20		Lt. THOMPSON R.A.M.C. reported for duty from E. Lancs Bn Eng. Owing to enemy retirement ordered from A.D.S. to send forward an Officer & means to keep in touch with Bde of 183 Bde. Then were in advance of division. Major RADFORD sent forward with detachment of bearers	Chl
	21		A.D.S. in S. Section moved forward to LE SART K27. d 3.2. with advanced post at K28 d 2.5. Capt TOBIAS in charge. Major RADFORD superintending evacuation from R.A.P.'s to A.D.S. at MEREDITH St., at K13 b 6.8. Large number of gas casualties (Yellow cross gas.)	Chl

Army Form C. 2118.

WAR DIARY
or
INTELLIGENCE SUMMARY.
(Erase heading not required.)

Instructions regarding War Diaries and Intelligence Summaries are contained in F. S. Regs., Part II. and the Staff Manual respectively. Title pages will be prepared in manuscript.

Place	Date	Hour	Summary of Events and Information	Remarks and references to Appendices
BOESEGHEM 17A83 Sheet 36A	Aug. 22		DMS V Army Maj General GERRARD visited Gas Centre.	Chl
	23		Relieved 2/2 Fd Amb. in forward area. Maj RADFORD RAMC in chg of MEREDITH ADS.	Chl
	24		Work of erecting NISSEN Huts at GAS Centre, BOESEGHEM. G.O.C. visited Gas Centre. 1 Casualty among 2/1 Fd Amb personnel from yellow cross gas, all slight.	Chl
HAVERSKERQUE J28d48	25		Headquarters moved forward to HAVERSKERQUE map ref J28 d.48. Transport lines and QM Stores remain at BOESEGHEM. Heavy thunderstorm rain.	Chl
	26		D.M.S. V Army. Major General GERRARD inspected Gas Centre. Continued wet weather.	Chl
	27		Work of repairing billets at HAVERSKERQUE continued also improvement of accommodation at G.S. Centre. Erection of form Nissen Hut completed there.	Chl
	28		ADS at MEREDITH St. enlarged & improved.	Chl
	29		DMS V Army visited ADS and HQrs. Continued showery weather. Order received from the Base to transfer Actg Serg Bailey PELLEY to 2/2 S.M. 2d Amb. as a Staff Sergt * in exchange with for Spr Maj Foss of 2/2 S M Fd Amb. Particulars sent to ADMS awake not completed with pending reply.	Chl
	30		Orders to carry retirement carparts advanced of ADds; party sent to leave post at MERVILLE at K.21 a.9.5. Lieut MacSWEENEY MRC returned from 2/2 S.M. 2d Amb.	Chl
	31		Conference at ADMS Office to discuss position of ADS and MDS in relation to forward area.	Chl

Chelenden Lt Col. R.A.M.C.
O/C 2/3rd Sm Field Ambulance

Medical 98/29
WO/3259

CONFIDENTIAL
WAR DIARY

OF

2/3rd South Midland Field Ambulance

From 1st September 1918 To 30th September 1918

(VOLUME _____)

2/3rd South Midland Field Ambulance

Committee Medical History
Date 9 Nov...

WAR DIARY or INTELLIGENCE SUMMARY

Army Form C. 2118.

MAPS. SHEETS 36 AND 36A.

Place	Date	Hour	Summary of Events and Information	Remarks and references to Appendices
HAVERSKERQUE T.25.d.4.8. Sheet 36c	Sep 1		MEREDITH A.D.S. handed over to 2/1st H. Amb. as M.D.S. A.D.S. established at MERVILLE with advanced car posts at L.26.D.27. and L.9.0. respectively	Col.
	2		R.A.Ps advanced to FAGGOT FM. L.23.d.3.9. & KENNET CROSS L.12.B.2.4. Sheet 36A. Reconnitred fr site for A.D.S. & H.Qrs. House selected at L.22.c.2.8. Orders issued to move A.D.S. from MERVILLE in the morning	Col
	3		A.D.S. moved forward to NEUF-BERQUIN — ESTAIRES Rd. Advd Post established at CHAPELLE-DUVELLE — ESTAIRES Rd. at L.28.c.9.4. Lieut THOMPSON MRC detached for duty with 9th Bn Northumberland Fusiliers.	Col
L.22.C.2.8	4		H.Qrs. moved from HAVERSKERQUE to NEUF-BERQUIN — ESTAIRES Rd. Gas Centre at BOESEGHEM ceased to admit gas cases. All cases sent to C.C.S. direct by order of D.M.S. 1st Army. Bridge over canal too at ESTAIRES completed. A.D.S. opened at SUCRERIE in NOUVEAU-MONDE	Col
	5		Car posted at SAILLY. Heavy thunder storms	Col.
	6		Gas Posted at night Left R.A.Ps. made very good recn of wounded t. A.D.S. lorry. Attached Pearston 24 S.M.Pd. Amb. returned to their Unit.	Col
	7		No. Cars a BOESEGHEM reduced to 43 by evacuation to C.C.S. of gas cases & of others to dup. + C.R.S.	Col
	8		Remaining patients at BOESEGHEM transferred to 2/2 Fd. Amb. at HAVERSKERQUE + STEENBECQUE. Construction of shelter at A.D.S. proceeding.	Col.

Army Form C. 2118.

WAR DIARY
or
INTELLIGENCE SUMMARY.
(Erase heading not required.)

Instructions regarding War Diaries and Intelligence Summaries are contained in F. S. Regs., Part II and the Staff Manual respectively. Title pages will be prepared in manuscript.

Place	Date	Hour	Summary of Events and Information	Remarks and references to Appendices
L22C 28 Sheet 36A	Sept 9		Major WOOD with personnel Q.M. Stores + transport + moved from BOESEGHEM to H.Qrs. a ESTAIRES—NEUF-BERQUIN Rd. Weather very wet.	C.M.
	10		Improving billets & accommodation at ADS	C.M.
	11		Repairing horses + making roads. Constantly showing men at ADS	C.M.
	12		Continued wet weather.	C.M.
	13		Routine duties at HR & ADS. Cleaning billets, repairing roads, &c.	C.M.
	14		Able received to prepare material for the Camphor preventive treatment of trench foot.	C.M.
	15		Order received to dispatch Capt. TOBIAS, Sr. R.A.M.C. to No 3 Cavalry cas. Depôt for duty. Fine weather. Cellar at ADS reported by RE office the suspected mined.	C.M.
	17		Lecture by ADMS. to requested M.O. at HO. Amb. HQ on Trench Foot Prevention.	C.M.
	18		Development of ADS in concrete building on canal bank proceeding.	C.M.
	19		Order received from D.H.Q. to evacuate ADS + hand over to the R.G.A. Arrangement made to establish ADS at G.26.d. 35.00	C.M. C.M. C.M.
	20		ADS moved from NOUVEAU MONDE to G.26.d.35.00. Showery weather.	C.M.
	21		Developing new ADS at G.26.d.35.00.	
	22		Commenced salary crop of bears in forward area making rick at HQrs	C.M.
	23		DMS order that all unpaid acting NCOs not authorised by DGMS should be reverted. Complied with.	C.M.

WAR DIARY
or
INTELLIGENCE SUMMARY
(Erase heading not required.)

Army Form C. 2118.

Place	Date	Hour	Summary of Events and Information	Remarks and references to Appendices
L22.c.2.8. Sturgen	Sept. 24.		Anti-aircraft Battery moved from A.D.S. Route work previously. Fine weather.	CHM
	26.		Lt.Col. LANDER proceeded on leave (U.K. Major WOOD took over temporary command of the Ambulance.	
	27.		Most of the personnel now employed assisting 147th Div. Sec. of the undermentioned lengths on the electricity R.E. Side framework of wood about 10ft × 3ft covered with canvas curved sheets of steel iron. The panels dug in to depth of about 3ft. Bullets controlled in the field forming the whole enveloping earth, leaving an entrance at one end. Routine duties.	
	28. 29.		Owing to increase of number of installations a line over a new host was formed by Major RADFORD o/c F.D.S. at H7.a.5.0. Short instructions were received from A.D.M.S. that in the event of a move forwards, the O.C. 2/1 S.M.A. would be responsible for clearing the right Brigade and O.C. 2/3 S.M.A. the left Brigade, the	

Army Form C. 2118.

WAR DIARY
INTELLIGENCE SUMMARY.
(Erase heading not required.)

Place	Date	Hour	Summary of Events and Information	Remarks and references to Appendices
Trenches Flers–Sea	Sept 29		District [?] line running through H.19 central. Thu? 3b. 4B seven [?] the attacked east [?] us [?] M.O. to 5 [?] seven [?] activity on our [?] station [?] in both Brigade units had full instructions. Acting on instructions the services [?] D.C. 2/S Suffolk & 2nd R.W.B. attacked seven [?] Battalion Rifle Brigade, & formed a lodgment post of N.C.O. & men abreast G.6.a.4.2 that 36.6 with a cov. The working party were afterwards relieved by an officer from 2/1 trench section [?] [?] [?] duties. Weather calm & fine.	vvvvvv vvvv vvv vvvvv vvv vvvv vvv v v vvv
	30			

W.V. Wood
Major Commanding
A.O.C. 2/3 [?]

CONFIDENTIAL

WAR DIARY

OF

2/3RD SOUTH MIDLAND FIELD AMBULANCE

FROM 1ST OCTOBER 1918 TO 31ST OCTOBER 1918

(VOLUME _____)

COMMITTEE FOR THE MEDICAL HISTORY OF THE WAR
Date 4 DEC 1918

2/3RD SOUTH MIDLAND FIELD AMBULANCE.
No.
Date.

WAR DIARY or INTELLIGENCE SUMMARY

Army Form C. 2118.

MAPS: Aub 2I.A. S.E. 5I.B Lens + Valenciennes

Place	Date	Hour	Summary of Events and Information	Remarks and references to Appendices
L.22.c.28.	Oct 1.		Routine duties.	
	2		O.C. 21 NC Field. 59 Sis, arranged arrange details of take over of trenches today. Our three + 30 men arrived advance party to commence relief of forward posts and ADS. Relief of post & advanced posts made by O.C. in all cars. Rain heavy. 2/2 N.C. had arrived at H.Q, opened when handed over, no casualties. Attached are three	
	3		2/2 & 2/1 F.A. hist of bulk of units at division on the boy routes, bath found unit, two lorries a bicycle sent ahead to frey our division on march at a specified location, move off by rest of Units of the Bpd. then rein our day to H.Q.R walked to Coyles. 10.30 Bpd at – STEENBECQUE. Ambulance entered transport with the exploits of trains of entrain Horse ambulances followed the Bpd. transport on march at 4.30 a.m. Good day's marching up Call out and arrived Steenbecque. Arrived Bpd at 4.30 p.m.	

A7692. Wt. W1128 g/M1293. 730,000. 11/17. D D & L, Ltd. Forms/C2118/14.

Army Form C. 2118.

WAR DIARY
or
INTELLIGENCE SUMMARY.
(Erase heading not required.)

Instructions regarding War Diaries and Intelligence Summaries are contained in F. S. Regs., Part II. and the Staff Manual respectively. Title pages will be prepared in manuscript.

Place	Date	Hour	Summary of Events and Information	Remarks and references to Appendices
ESTRÉES-EN-CHAUSSÉE STEENBECQUE	Oct 4		Brigade sick externals (remainder) to CCS at MRE. Wagons, harness & equipment cleaned. Allotments of training systems & continental billets.	
"	5		Route march 9-12 (Personal orders received for transfer to Second Army detachment). [General Thompson (Adjutant) to C.C. (Hatting Party) am & next moment. Lt THOMPSON detailed as M.O. for entraining station & to two cars. Duties commencing 11 pm. 5.10.18.	
	6.		Mostly train STEENBECQUE to DOULLENS. Marched to BEITVREPAIRE 4 kilos outside DOULLENS in the DOULLENS-ARRAS road. Very fine weather. Transferred from XI. Corps X. Army to XVII Corps III Army. Lt THOMPSON returns at 5 later (7:15 pm Picq) by LT McSWEENEY	
BEAURAPAIRE	7.		Routine camp duties. Lt McSWEENEY reported with the one truck transport and one limber wagon etc. arrived at number WMR	
	8.		RADFORD & Lt THOMPSON. Gun establishment, 3 days march	

Army Form C. 2118.

WAR DIARY
or
INTELLIGENCE SUMMARY.
(Erase heading not required.)

Instructions regarding War Diaries and Intelligence Summaries are contained in F. S. Regs., Part II. and the Staff Manual respectively. Title pages will be prepared in manuscript.

Place	Date	Hour	Summary of Events and Information	Remarks and references to Appendices
BEAUREPAIRE DEVIATION	Oct 9		Personnel marched train from MONDICOURT to HERMIES. Marched to camp area J.7.c.cent. map 57.c. Bivouacked in dugouts & trench shelters.	
T.J.C.Cent Map 57c	10		Transport arrived. Commenced trekking for XVII Corps Rest Station from 2/3 Wessex Field Amb. 57 Div. Replaced them personnel, kept continuously on duty.	
	11		Ambulances ditto from 61 Div and attached to XVIII Corps as special duty, mainly clearing of experimental station. The camp is on waste nd of 14 main[?] roads & to Bell observation stations. for 350 patients. Wounded were in shelters. Prisoners casualties mainly of lightly wounded men from CORPS MAIN DRESSING STATION. 310 patients were transferred to rear by No 2/3 & No 3/3 West Sussex F. Amb. B	

Army Form C. 2118.

WAR DIARY
or
INTELLIGENCE SUMMARY.

(Erase heading not required.)

Instructions regarding War Diaries and Intelligence Summaries are contained in F. S. Regs., Part II. and the Staff Manual respectively. Title pages will be prepared in manuscript.

Place	Date	Hour	Summary of Events and Information	Remarks and references to Appendices
T.Y.C. Sheet 57c	Oct. 12		Lt.Col. C.L. LANDER returned from leave and resumed command.	ChL
	13		Routine duties	ChL
	14		Major RADFORD rode to ADMS office via Major BOLDERO on leave. Lieut McSWEENEY sent to GOUY in charge of service to patients there. C.O. visited CAMBRAI with a view to speak C.R.S. at College de NOTRE-DAME-de GRACE	ChL
	15		Sick cases transported from GOUY by M.A.C. cars to T.Y.C. with 6 sitting cases but others. Advance party sent on to CAMBRAI Scabies patients moved to CAMBRAI by MT ambulance 3.30 & la FOLIE FARM.	ChL ChL
	16		moved to College de GRACE. Everything ready. Others moved from T.Y.C. to College d GRACE. Lt McSWEENEY detailed for duty with 2/5 Gloucest. Bn. to relieve Capt. GLEED same.	ChL
CAMBRAI A16a 7.2. Sheet 57d	17		C.R.S. opened at midnight 16-17th at COLLEGE de GRACE. CRS patients members to light railway returned to la FOLIE FARM under Lt. THOMPSON MRC where they were arranged by M.A.C. to new C.R.S. Ambulance personnel TKC moved to new CRS has now party under Major WOOD to load while + strike the camp. 10 G.S. Wagon loads (tents attached from 2/1, 2/2 Fd Amb) and 8 lorry loads sent on to CAMBRAI Capt GLEED joined from 2/5 Gloucester via Lt McSWEENEY MCC DDMS XIII Corps visited CRS and made a tour of inspection.	ChL

WAR DIARY or INTELLIGENCE SUMMARY

Army Form C. 2118.

Place	Date	Hour	Summary of Events and Information	Remarks and references to Appendices
CAMBRAI A16 c/7.2 Sht 57 B	Oct. 18		Capt Lieut STONE RAMC SR detailed for duty with RE's to relieve Capt RENNIE RAMC. Two lorry load of material moved from J.J.C. to camp RCA1	Chl
	19		Capt RENNIE RAMS taken on the Strength of the Ambulance. Three MAC lorries sent to COY's clean station there + two to T.T.O. the latter did a double journey + cleared Beaver Division of 42nd D Cas. provided with billets at COLLEGE NOTRE DAME de GRACE the camp. Patients moved about 400. 12 SB officers in M.I. room	Chl
	20		Organisation of CRS proceeds. Patient numbers about 200. detailed to convey Cam. to CCS at LA FOLIE F.VIC.	Chl
	21		Routine duties. Repairs premises. One NCO + two men	Chl
	22		SDMS XVII Corps visited CRS. Heavy admissions due to Influenza. 198 h. numbers placed for civilian	Chl
	23		Beaver Division convey of S.R. BUXTON + 46 O.R. marched to AVESNES lez AUBERT by Capt RENNIE to duty in forward area & with 2 S.M.Fd. Amb. No admissions. 176	Chl
	24		Capt MACDONALD of XVII Corps [strikethrough] for temporary duty to assist in the afternoon. Heavy admission numbers 316. In the absence of MAC Cars Horsed Ambulances + GS Wagons were used to convey cases to the L.f.r. railway at LA FOLIE FAIE. during the day 237	Chl
25			Number of cases admitted 195. Discharged to duty 41. To CCS 101	Chl
	26			do 221 do 59 do 153 Capt MAYES returned from leave	Chl
	27			SDMS visited Ground Medical Ward. Orders received to institute the name XVII CORPS SICK COLLECTING STATION for XVII CORPS REST. STATION. All the Ambulance Cars sent to 21st Field Ambly. Two MAC Cars attached to CSCS for Evacuations	Chl

Army Form C. 2118.

WAR DIARY
or
INTELLIGENCE SUMMARY.
(Erase heading not required.)

Instructions regarding War Diaries and Intelligence Summaries are contained in F. S. Regs., Part II and the Staff Manual respectively. Title pages will be prepared in manuscript.

Place	Date	Hour	Summary of Events and Information	Remarks and references to Appendices
CAMBRAI AREA	Oct 28		Routine duties. Admissions 190. Evacuations Totals 114 to CCS 131. Remaining 709	CWL
	29		Capt MILNER R.A.M.C reported for duty in stead of Capt McDONALD R.A.M.C. Been absent returned from 21st S.M. Bd and DAH. cleaning up holly road now continued. Admissions 232.	CWL
	30		Discharges to duty 113. 6 CCS 152. Remaining 658.	CWL
	31		Routine duties. Confined for month.	CWL

M. C. Phillip
Commanding 73rd S.M. Field Ambulance

MEDICAL 9831

CONFIDENTIAL
WAR DIARY
OF
2/3rd. South Midland Field Ambulance

FROM 1st November 1918 TO 30th November 1918

(VOLUME _____)

MAPS LENS 11.
CAMBRAI.

Army Form C. 2118.

WAR DIARY
or
INTELLIGENCE SUMMARY.
(Erase heading not required.)

Place	Date	Hour	Summary of Events and Information	Remarks and references to Appendices
CAMBRAI	Nov 1		Preparations completed. Known up to 1000 Sick & Slightly Wounded at C.C.C.S	Chl
COLLEGE NOIRE DES. DE BRAIT			Capt. SATOW R.A.M.C. at 19.O.R. from 62nd Fd. Amb. attached for duty.	Chl
	2		Maj. RADFORD R.A.M.C. returned from Div. H.Q.	
			Admissions 272 Discharge to duty 35 to CCS 147 Remaining 859	Chl
	3		Admissions 255 do do 91 do 201 do 822 Routine duties	Chl
	4		Lt. METZGER M.R.C. VIIth Aus. reported for duty to relieve Capt SATOW R.A.M.C 62nd Amb.	Chl
			Admissions 240 Discharge to duty 95 to CCS 127 Remaining 840	Chl
			Admissions 239 Discharge to duty 71 to CCS 155 Remaining 873	Chl
	5		Lt. McSWEENEY M.R.C. returned to duty with 1st Aus. on discharge from C.C.C.S.	
	6		Admissions 278 Discharge to duty 92 to CCS 139 Remaining 920	Chl
	7		Admissions 236 Discharge to duty 89 to CCS 234 Remaining 833	Chl
	8		Admissions 243 Discharge to duty 21 to CCS 190 Remaining 859	Chl
	9		Admissions 188 Discharge to duty 89 to CCS 113 Remaining 845 30 CCS Tents	Chl
			Sent to Field Ambulance at AVESNES for use as entraining point for Sick cases. Coming from forward Area	
	10		DELSAUX FARM Group of CCCS closed all CCS cases sent to AWOINGT G.S.W.	Chl
			Admissions 94 Discharge to duty 95 to CCS 76 Remaining 768	Chl

Army Form C. 2118.

WAR DIARY
or
INTELLIGENCE SUMMARY.
(Erase heading not required)

Place	Date	Hour	Summary of Events and Information	Remarks and references to Appendices
CAMBRAI Collecting Pst. Place de Gaul	Nov. 10		Arrangement completed to receive sick & train for ST AUBERT at CAMBRAI ANNEXE Pte. on leave attached; Admissions 94 Discharge to duty 95 to CCS 46 Remaining 469	Ch.
	11		News received from XVII Corps of cessation of hostilities at 11:00 hours today. Admissions 96 Discharge to duty 163 to CCS 51 Remaining 350 Major RADFORD proceeds on leave to PARIS	Ch.
	12		Order received to evacuate all cases with exception of duty with a few days. Admissions 104 Discharge to duty 79 to CCS 125 Remaining 692 to 137 Amb. 18	Ch. Ch.
	13		Admissions 58 Discharge to duty 70 to CCS 74 Remaining 606	Ch.
	14		Order received to evacuate sick to ANOINGT Group CCS Admissions 115 Discharge to duty 82 to CCS 208 Remaining 431	Ch.
	15		Admissions 23 Discharge to duty 181 to CCS 27 Remaining 259 246	Ch.
	16		Corps store of blanket stretchers &c. sent to Army Ordnance under DDMS orders. Admissions ceased under Corps order. Discharge to duty 185 to CCS 14 Remaining 58 Works Adm[inistratio]n close to Bidwand and supervy of BR Estab. taken over by Col. Starr assisted Lt. METZGER M.C. U.S.A. Acquired 61st Fd. Amb. Tel. Subdvision of 132nd Fd. Amb. returned today.	Ch.
	17		Discharge to duty 50 to CCS 10 Remaining Nil Sgt. R. Buttmann[?] etc confined The M.O. can returned to their H.O. One Officers charge at R.S. where he was to be kept 5 [?] Pte. Capa	Ch. Ch. Pte Capa

WAR DIARY
or
INTELLIGENCE SUMMARY

Army Form C. 2118.

Place	Date	Hour	Summary of Events and Information	Remarks and references to Appendices
CAMBRAI Collg Notre Dame de Grace	Nov. 18		Corps Sick Collecting Pt closed at 0600 hrs. All cases sent to 3rd H.Q. S/TREASURE awarded M.M.	C/LL
	19		Parade of Camp personnel in marching order. Opened as 3rd Ambulance for Sick & Stragglers. Truck Officers	C/LL
	20		Inspection of Horse Transport	C/LL
	21		Routine duties	C/LL
			Lt. Col. GRAY Dermatologist to 5th Army visited Langemarck Section opp. Odds Work Division at CAMBRAI in charge of XVII Corps Sick when 61 beds were	C/LL
	22		When readying Athens to detach one with Ambulance during move of 39th to Mr D.A.C. and to take medical charge of entrance at CAMBRAI VILLE on 24" 4"25" Nov.	C/LL
	23		Order received from DDMS XVII Corps to send one section and a car to BEUGNATRE (Sheet LENS 11 K.5.) One Officer 8 O.R. & 2 cars to COIGNEUX (Sheet LENS 11 G.5) One Section to HAPLINCOURT (Sheet LENS 11 L.5) One Section to ALBERT (Sheet LENS 11 H.6) Three M.A.C. Cars reported for duty. To evacuate sick & troops marching through & 56 CCS PREVILLERS & 43 CCS BEAULENCOURT.	C/LL
HAPLINCOURT Sheet LENS 11 L5	24		Ambulance moved off complete at 8 a.m. and marched A & B Section to HAPLINCOURT. C Section to BEUGNATRE. Lt. THOMPSON in charge at BEUGNATRE. Capt GLEED at COIGNEUX Capt RENNIE at ALBERT. H.Qrs at HAPLINCOURT. Capt GLEED moved to BIENVILLERS for COIGNEUX	C/LL
ALBERT	25		A. Section moved to ALBERT. Capt RENNIE returned to take charge of B Section at HAPLINCOURT	C/LL
	26		LT. THOMPSON M.C. USA promoted to CAPTAIN. Major M.V. WOOD returned from leave.	C/LL

Army Form C. 2118.

WAR DIARY
or
INTELLIGENCE SUMMARY.
(Erase heading not required.)

Instructions regarding War Diaries and Intelligence Summaries are contained in F. S. Regs., Part II. and the Staff Manual respectively. Title pages will be prepared in manuscript.

Place	Date	Hour	Summary of Events and Information	Remarks and references to Appendices
ALBERT (LENS H)	Nov 27		Routine duties. Improving billets, meet constructing hut huts latrines &c. Orders received relaxing censorship regulations as regards information allowed in letters, also relation to	CMC
	28		Rations for A Section did not arrive from 20th Div as ordered by XVIII Corps.	CMC CMC
	29		Relieve arrival of B+C Section Attack Stores for next Div sector. Wiring order received to prepare Div for Dec 2.18	CMC
	30		Routine duties. Battery relaying kit. Capt THOMPSON M.C. U.S.A. sent on leave to England.	CMC

C Wadle
Lt. Col. RMC
O/C D/S Smith Army

Medical

CONFIDENTIAL

War Diary

of

2/3RD SOUTH MIDLAND FIELD AMBULANCE.

From 1ST DECEMBER 1918 To 31ST DECEMBER 1918.

(VOLUME)

WAR DIARY or INTELLIGENCE SUMMARY

Army Form C. 2118.

MAPS: LENS.

Place	Date	Hour	Summary of Events and Information	Remarks and references to Appendices
ALBERT (LENS 6A 81)	Dec. 1		Maj. RADFORD returned from leave.	CHL
PUCHEVILLERS LENS	3		A Section marched to PUCHEVILLERS billeted in PW Camp E of village. B Section under Maj. WOOD moved to ALBERT. C Section under Maj. RADFORD moved to ALBERT.	CHL
	4		B & C Sections rejoined unit at PUCHEVILLERS.	CHL
	6		Order received from ADMS to move to BERNAVILLE pending more permanent location.	CHL
BERNAVILLE 6.D.96	7		Unit marched to BERNAVILLE billeted in huts W of Village.	CHL
MESNIL DOMQUEUR 5A 9.6.	8		Marched to MESNIL DOMQUEUR & took over billets & small hospital from 2/2 S.M. 2d Amb. Order recd for 118 Bde at 2100 hours to move to billets in DOMART on the 9th.	CHL
DOMART 6B59	9		Marched to billets in DOMART-EN-PONTHIEU. Maj. RADFORD & Capt. GLEED with small detachment of C Section left in charge of hospital at MESNIL DOMQUEUR. Capt. RENNIE proceeded to PARIS on leave.	CHL
	10		Improving billets which consist of a building formerly used as a laundry by 63 Div. Horse transport scattered in billets about the village. Educated clean commenced on Trench Mycology. Building suitable for hospital secured.	CHL
	12			CHL
	13		Hospital closed at MESNIL DOMQUEUR and opened at DOMART at billet 150. Field Ambulance football team won the first round in the Divl Sports defeating B Coy. of the R. Berks R.R.	CHL
	14		Routine duties. Major General DUNCAN visited the hospital & inspected the billets &c.	CHL
	16		ADMS inspected billets & hospital.	CHL
	17		Capt. THOMPSON M.C. USA and Capt. RENNIE RAMC returned from leave. Football team defeated C Coy. of the R Berks Batt in the second round of Divl Contest.	CHL

WAR DIARY
or
INTELLIGENCE SUMMARY.
(Erase heading not required.)

Army Form C. 2118.

Place	Date	Hour	Summary of Events and Information	Remarks and references to Appendices
DOMART-EN-PONTHIEU (LENS 6859)	Dec 19		Capt MAYES proceeded on special leave to England	CM
	20		Capt. RENNIE RAMC detailed for duty with 9" Northumberland Fusiliers. Capt. THOMPSON MC VSA sent to relieve Capt. BELL of 306 Bde. RFA going on leave in France. 15 O.R. despatched to 18 CCS DOULLENS for duty.	CM
	21		Lt. THOMSON MC VSA reported for duty for 9" Northumberland Fusiliers Bn.	CM
	22		Routine duties.	CM
	23		XVII Corps War received reference immediate demobilisation of Officers & men on leave who have guaranteed employment, and are not essential to their military unit. ADMS visited Ambulance in special Hospital &c.	CM
	25		Christmas day. Little effect on short football competition between the Sections. HT, MT & SC. Victory of B Section. Dinner at 1800 hours consisting of Pork and Goose. Plum pudding first rate. followed by impromptu "concert" in DOMART HALL with 104 Bde H.Q. Fine frosty day. Sgt Major Pellé + St Brown go on leave. Warrants not asked to return first."	CM
	26		Lt. THOMSON MC VSA detailed for temporary duty with 315 Bde. RFA. Sgt Sgt WILKINS reported as Sgt Major.	CM
	27		Major RADFORD MC RAMC proceeded on leave to PARIS to purchase toys for 104 Bde Entertainment to french children. No 15 MT Ambulance Car partially destroyed by fire. Dr JENKINS + a patient injured.	CM

Army Form C. 2118.

WAR DIARY
or
INTELLIGENCE SUMMARY.

(Erase heading not required.)

Instructions regarding War Diaries and Intelligence Summaries are contained in F. S. Regs., Part II. and the Staff Manual respectively. Title pages will be prepared in manuscript.

Place	Date	Hour	Summary of Events and Information	Remarks and references to Appendices
DONAI (Sheet 51 B 5/9)	Dec 28		Field Ambulance football team defeat 479 Coy RE in Divisional contest	Ctd.
	29		Five miners despatched from unit to CAMBRAI for demobilisation. Routine duties	Ctd.
	30		Field Ambulance football team defeated by 183rd Bde HQ Team by 2 goals to nil in Divisional contest.	Ctd.
	31		Routine duties.	Ctd.

Olanda
W.G.R.A.R.C
O/c 2/3rd S.M. Field Ambulance

2/3RD
SOUTH MIDLAND
FIELD AMBULANCE.

MEDICAL

WO 95/34

145/5440

CONFIDENTIAL

61st Div Bot 2929

WAR DIARY

OF

2/3rd SOUTH MIDLAND FIELD AMBULANCE

From 1st January 1919 to 31st January 1919.

Volume

WAR DIARY or INTELLIGENCE SUMMARY

Army Form C.

Place	Date	Hour	Summary of Events and Information	Remarks and references to Appendices
DOMART EN PONTHIEU (LENS. 6.B.59)	JAN 1 1919		Routine duties. A. Section dinner tonight.	Ch.
	2		Sgt. BUXTON & one O.R. detailed for duty at XVII Corps Demobilisation Camp in CANDAS-MONTRELET.	Ch. Ch.
	3		Capt. P. THOMPSON M.C. U.S.A. returned from 306 Bde R.F.A.	Ch.
	4		Capt. MAYES returned from leave. C. Section dinner tonight. Field Amb. football team defeats Officers + North B. Team 2 goals - 1 goal.	Ch.
	5		Inspection of and classification of transport animals by D.A.D.V.S.	Ch.
	6		Sgt. LEWIS & 1 O.R. proceed to XVII Corps Concentration Camp for demobilisation. Copy of report of D.A.D.V.S. to 61 Div. D.Q. received on condition of transport animals in 2/1 Field Ambulance - Very good - useful creation on all concerned.	Ch.
	7		Capt. S. R. GLEED R.A.M.C. returned from leave.	Ch.
	8		III Army letter received Cancelling demobilisation of men on leave who proceed on or after the 12th inst.	Ch.
	9		Routine duties	Ch.
	10		Leave allotment now cancelled	Ch.
	11		Hospital and billets re-inspected by D.D.M.S. XVII Corps.	Ch.
	12		Routine duties	Ch.
	14		Classification + inspection of horse mules by Divisional Remount Officer as follows X. 6. (1HD. 4.M. 1 R.da.) Y 25. (13 HD. 9LD 3 Riders) Z. 12. (5 HD. 4 M. 3 Riders)	Ch.
	16		Routine duties	Ch.
	18		Instructions received that D.H.S. Army had decided to limit the demobilisation of O.R. of field Ambulances to 30% with Officers @ demobilisation is ordered. Demobilisation then to proceed at the rate of 10% per week until reduced to 1 Section per field Ambulance. No M.O. to be released without sanction of D.H.S.	Ch.

Army Form C.2118

WAR DIARY
or
INTELLIGENCE SUMMARY.
(Erase heading not required.)

Instructions regarding War Diaries and Intelligence Summaries are contained in F.S. Regs., Part II. and the Staff Manual respectively. Title pages will be prepared in manuscript.

Place	Date	Hour	Summary of Events and Information	Remarks and references to Appendices
DOMART EN-PONTHIEU (LENS 1 B 55)	Jan 20		Played 2/r SM FA and at AGENVILLE at football Scored 2-1 against us. About 50 O.R. remained to the review afterwards on the invitation of Lt Col BURROUGHES	Col
	21		Copy of War Establishment of a Field Ambulance received from ADMS. The new establishment consists of two Sections, total personnel 211, horses 34, Motor Ambulances 7. Horse Ambulances 2.	Col
	23		Routine duties	Col
	24		Capt. THOMPSON M.C. U.S.A. detailed to duty temporarily with 6 Northumberland Fusiliers	Col
	25		Capt GLEED RAMC detailed for temporary duty with 11th Suffolks. The following awards are in the London Gazette published – Bar to Order Hospers Thomas D.S.O. Capt (acti/Lt Col) C.L. LANDER RAMC	Col
	27		Routine duties	Col
	28		Orders received from ADMS to send 12 Pts & 2 Cpls to report to DDMS ROUEN on the 30th for duty. A/M.S.TOLLEY to report to ADMS ABBEVILLE like in connection with Base Depot of Med Stores.	Col
	30		The above mentioned personnel despatched in accordance with instructions to hand 1/2 the strength of the Unit, with the exception that Q.M.S TOLLEY preceded with the party to ROUEN	Col
	29		Major W.V. WOOD A.C. RAMC proceeded to England on Special Leave	Col

Alexander M Col RAMC
O/C 73rd S.W. Field Amb Co

MEDICAL
98/34

CONFIDENTIAL

WAR DIARY

OF

2/3rd SOUTH MIDLAND FIELD AMBULANCE

From 1st FEBRUARY to 28th FEBRUARY 1919.

(VOLUME   )

(LENS 6359)
(ABBEVILLE 5193)

Army Form C. 2118.

WAR DIARY
or
INTELLIGENCE SUMMARY.
(Erase heading not required.)

Instructions regarding War Diaries and Intelligence Summaries are contained in F. S. Regs., Part II. and the Staff Manual respectively. Title pages will be prepared in manuscript.

Place	Date	Hour	Summary of Events and Information	Remarks and references to Appendices
DOMART-EN-PONTHIEU (LENS 6359)	Feb 1		3 HD lorries & 1 D hirer sent to DIEPPE Base Remount Depot under orders of ADMS	CM
	2		Routine duties	CM
	3		The only remaining motor ambulance with the unit have have been removed to workshops for repair	CM
	4		Motor ambulance detailed for duty daily for 2/1 S.H.Fd. Aml.	CM
	5		Routine duties	CM
	7		The motor ambulance returned from workshops to this unit.	CM
	8		Capt GLEED RAMC & Capt P. THOMPSON MC VPS struck off the strength of this Ambulance	CM
	9		The following acting appointments were recommended & forwarded to complete establishment Sp! CUFF H b/e Q.M.S. &Sgt KAINES Cpl A.J STOCK L/Cpl A.RUMMINGS & L/Cpl W.SIBLEY to be Sergeants. H/Cpls WILMOT & HIRON and Ptes F.C PEARCE J.S.SMITH W.CLARK & V.WHEELER to be Corporals Pte A.H.WILLIAMS & RUMMINGS b/e L/a C Corporals Spl HIGHAM b/e Staff Sergeant.	CM
	11		Authority received from the W.O for demobilisation of Capt Art H.Col C.L.LAUDER RAMCTF and Major A.RADFORD RAMCTF at the earliest possible date	CM
	12		Orders received from ADMS to move to billets at BUSSUS-BUSUEL on the 13th	CM
BUSSUS-BUSUEL (Abbeville 5193)	13		Unit marched to BUSSUS-BUSSUEL with as much equipment as there were horses available for	CM
	14		Remainder of equipment & vehicle brought on from DOMART & also stores Ordnance & RE dispatched in lorries to CANOTS at DOMLEGER respectively.	CM
	15		MAJOR W.V.WOOD RAMC returned from leave Capt M. SOMERVILLE RAMC T.C. taken on the strength & temporarily attached to No. 47 Labour Group for duty	CM

WAR DIARY or INTELLIGENCE SUMMARY

Army Form C. 2118.

Place	Date	Hour	Summary of Events and Information	Remarks and references to Appendices
BUSSUS-BUSSUEL (ABBEVILLE 51.9b)	Feb. 19.		Lt Col LANDER DSO MC & Maj. RADFORD MC proceed to England for demobilization.	
	20.		Maj WOOD takes over command of the Ambulance.	
	23.		Routine duties.	
	24.		Game taken at the village school (in use by us) went into return receipt. Whist drive between Sergts + Men. Lieut Hett Granted 10 days leave (Paris). Lt Col LANDER DSO MC (MajSurgeon) ordered to rejoin unit - section 11 CDS 384 December October 1918 to wear letters of rank of LtCol	
	25.		Capt (a/Major WOOD)	
	26.		Routine duties	
	27.		Men sent on detached duty to 78 CCS unit to be off strength of this unit 57 men 1 Lieut unit have now (are demobilised).	
	28.		Routine duties	

W J Wood
Lt Col RAMC

WAR DIARY

OF

2/3rd South Midland Field Ambulance

FROM March 1st 1919 TO March 31st 1919.

(VOLUME ......)

ABBEVILLE 14
LENS 11

WAR DIARY
or
INTELLIGENCE SUMMARY.
(Erase heading not required.)

Army Form C. 2118.

Place	Date	Hour	Summary of Events and Information	Remarks and references to Appendices
BUSSUS BUSSUEL			Sent list of allotment for the month. Three places say took	"""
			day in Rane period. Moved to A.S.C. very little to do.	"""
ABBEVILLE 1919.			Transport out – but the horses are kept up in fair condition.	"""
Lens. II.			Rations very in quantity. Washing in poor.	"""
	6.		Nothing of general interest. Capt W.N.BELL RAMC applied to	"""
			duty, was taken on the strength.	"""
	10.		Orders were received for MAJOR W.V.WOOD to be demobilized	"""
			from DIEPPE D. MAJOR WOOD stated that he was unwilling to	"""
			be demobilised at present.	"""
	12.		CAPT BELL struck off ration strength on leave to U.K.	"""
	19		Major W.V.Wood proceeded to TUB for Demobilization and Major	Att
			G. Simson took this Unit over from H.Q. Staff and assumed command	Att
			Major W.V.Wood shewed signs of strength	Att
	20		Instructions received that Cadre of Unit will move to be depot on 27/3/19 falling in	Att
	23		at Abbeville.	Att
	24		Units Staff Improving in num-	Att
	25		Suns Staff improving by Search parties. Stayed at Frevenville.	Att
	26		Commenced move by Search parties.	Att
			Completed March to be Depot without incident.	Att

ABBEVILLE 14.

Army Form C. 2118.

WAR DIARY
or
INTELLIGENCE SUMMARY.
(Erase heading not required.)

Place	Date	Hour	Summary of Events and Information	Remarks and references to Appendices
Le Hupot	29		Cleaning up and arranging Medical Inspection Room & Camp	A17
	30		Major A.P. Thomson proceeds to U.K. on leave. Capt. A. Dun Waters assumes Temporary Command of Unit.	A19
	31		Capt. W.M. St. Clair rejoins from Leave in U.K. after 3 days extension.	111916

Confidential

War Diary
of
2/3rd South Midland Field Ambulance

From 1st April 1919.
To 30th April 1919.

(VOLUME   )

17 JUL 1919

Army Form C. 2118.

WAR DIARY
or
INTELLIGENCE SUMMARY
(Erase heading not required.)

MORVILLE
2/3RD
SOUTH MIDLAND
FIELD AMBULANCE.

No 36

Place	Date	Hour	Summary of Events and Information	Remarks and references to Appendices
LE TREPORT	1/4/19		Major J.P. Thomson proceeds to England on 1 months leave and leave pending Demobilisation. C. Mayo assumes temporary command of the Unit.	WD
	2/4/19		Captain W.H. McDell returned from leave in United Kingdom and assumed Command of Unit	WD
	3/4/19 to 26/4/19		During this period ordinary routine duties were carried out. Here being nothing of interest to report.	WD
	27/4/19		Captain Auckinvale C. Mayo proceeds to England on 14 days leave	WD
	28/4/19 to 30/4/19		Routine Duties	

W.H.M^c D
Captain Lane
O.C. 2/3 S.M. Field Ambulance

2/3rd S. Ind. Field Amb.

ABBEVILLE

2/3 S.M. Fd Amb

Army Form C. 2118.

WAR DIARY
or
INTELLIGENCE SUMMARY.
(Erase heading not required.)

Instructions regarding War Diaries and Intelligence Summaries are contained in F. S. Regs., Part II. and the Staff Manual respectively. Title pages will be prepared in manuscript.

Place	Date	Hour	Summary of Events and Information	Remarks and references to Appendices
Le TREPORT	May 1		to Troops	
	3		The Town of Le Tréport was placed out of bounds until 1800 hours on account of French revolt day	Ok
	6		Lieut/Col. H.P. Thomson returned from leave in U.K.	Ok
	13		Captain W.H. Bell posted to 4th Royal Bucks Regt.	Ok
	15		Captain W. Mayo rejoined from leave in U.K.	Ok
	26		Lieut Col. O.P. Thomson posted to No. 2 Infirmary Hospital, ABBEVILLE + Capt Mayo	Ok
			assumed Command of Unit. Inauguration of Foreign Service of this Unit.	Ok
				Ok
			With the Exception of items mentioned above Saturday has been occupied by Routine Duties in morning continued with Recreation in afternoon.	Ok

C. Mayo
Captain Comm'd'g
2/3rd South Midland Fd Amb'ce

2/3RD
SOUTH MIDLAND
FIELD AMBULANCE.
No. ....
Date ....

140/3601

22 SEP 1919

June 1919

WAR DIARY
or
INTELLIGENCE SUMMARY.
(Erase heading not required.)

Army Form C. 2118.

Le Treport.

Place	Date	Hour	Summary of Events and Information	Remarks and references to Appendices
Le Treport.	June.			
	June 1.		Routine Work. All harness dismantled, cleaned oiled and tied together in sections and returned to stores in readiness for packing on G.S.Wagons.	
	6.		Cadre Strenght of this Unit reduced by 75%, and personnel sent to dispersal camp for demob'	
	12.		General Routine work.	
	16.		Equipment cleaned labelled and packed under supervision of Capt. Mayes and loaded on Wagons, sheeted and roped and ready for embarkation.	
	26		Inspection of Camp premises and billets by Officer Commanding. Routine work.	
	27		Routine work and cleaning of personal equipment.	
			With the exception of items mentioned above each day has been occupied by Routine Duties in the morning coupled with Recreation in afternoon.	

Chzyele..............Capt.RAMC.T.

Comdg. 2/3 1st Sth Mid Fld Ambce. (Equipment Guard.

2/3RD
SOUTH MIDLAND
FIELD AMBULANCE.
No.
Date. 10/7/19

COMMITTEE FOR THE
3 SEP 1919
MEDICAL HISTORY OF THE WAR

Army Form C. 2118.

WAR DIARY
or
INTELLIGENCE SUMMARY.
(Erase heading not required.)

Place	Date	Hour	Summary of Events and Information	Remarks and references to Appendices
Le Treport	July.			
	July	3.	Routine Work. Cleaning and Oiling Wagons.	
		8.	Wagons un-roped and Equipment examined.	
		12.		
		13.	General Routine Work.	
		14.		
		20.	Wagons stencilled ready for Embarkation. (2/3rd S.M.Fld.Amb. Aintree.)	
		24.	Inspection of Camp premises and billets by the O.C.	
		26.		
		27.	General Routine Work.	
		28.		

..............Capt. RAMC.(T).
Comdg., 2/3rd South Midland Field Ambulance.
(Equipment Guard)

2/3RD SOUTH MIDLAND FIELD AMBULANCE.

www.ingramcontent.com/pod-product-compliance
Lightning Source LLC
Chambersburg PA
CBHW080904230426
43664CB00016B/2722